flaminio gundy

Jesolo Lido
Sand, sand and sand

JESOLO LIDO
Sand, sand and sand

by Flaminio Gundy

All rights reserved.
No part of this book may be used or reproduced in any manner without written permission of the publisher.

Copyright © 2018 Flaminio Gundy

Createspace Independent Publishing, Charleston, South Carolina, USA, 2018

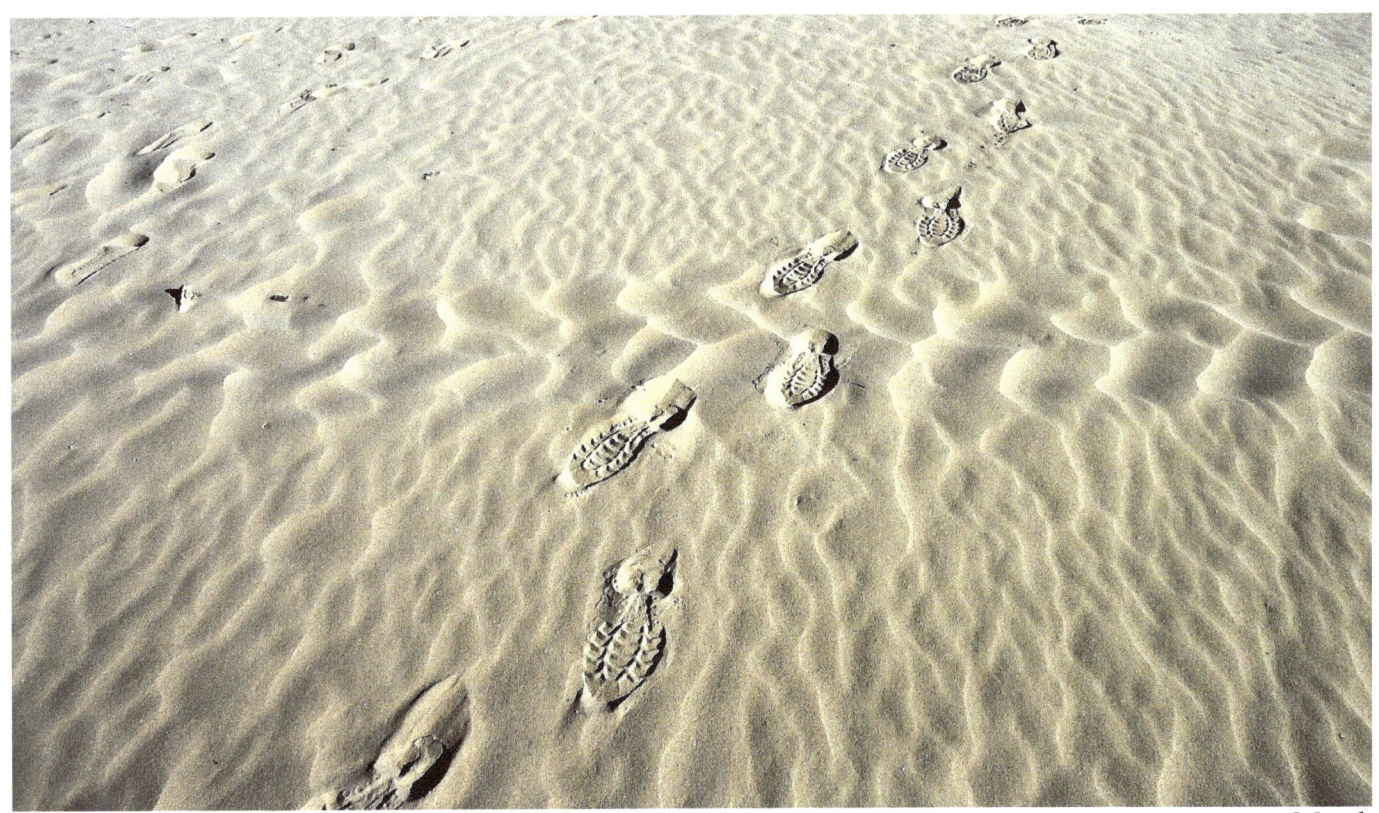

March

Alici marinate, *marinated anchovies*. Disembowel a dozen anchovies (or sardines) until you get two whole fillets each. Wash them, dry them well and place them side by side in a large saucepan. Cut an onion and a clove of garlic into thin wedges and pour them over the fish. Squeeze two lemons almost to cover the fillets, then sprinkle with parsley and ground pepper. Cover the saucepan with a sheet of transparent film, make a few holes with a toothpick and place it in the fridge for 3 hours, or even longer if the fillets are thick. Once marinated, remove them, drain them from their sauce and dry them well. Arrange them on a tray, pour a little oil and season with salt and pepper.

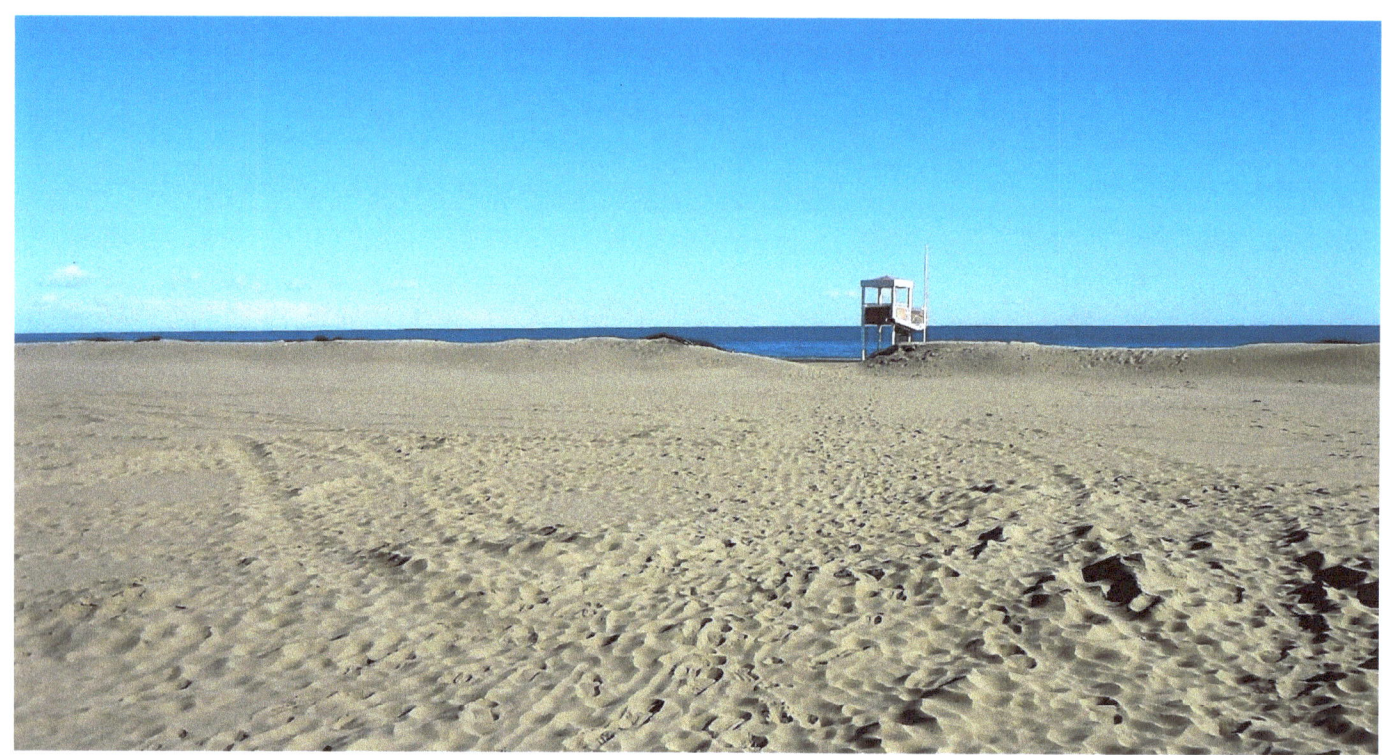

March

Canestrelli in forno, *queen scallops in the oven*. Open the shells of the queen scallops leaving the mollusc attached and wash them well in running water to remove the sand. Fry two cloves of garlic in the oil to give it flavor. Fill each shell with a little breadcrumbs, two drops of oil flavored with garlic, salt, pepper and a pinch of parsley. Place the stuffed shells in an oven dish and bake in a hot oven for no longer than five minutes.

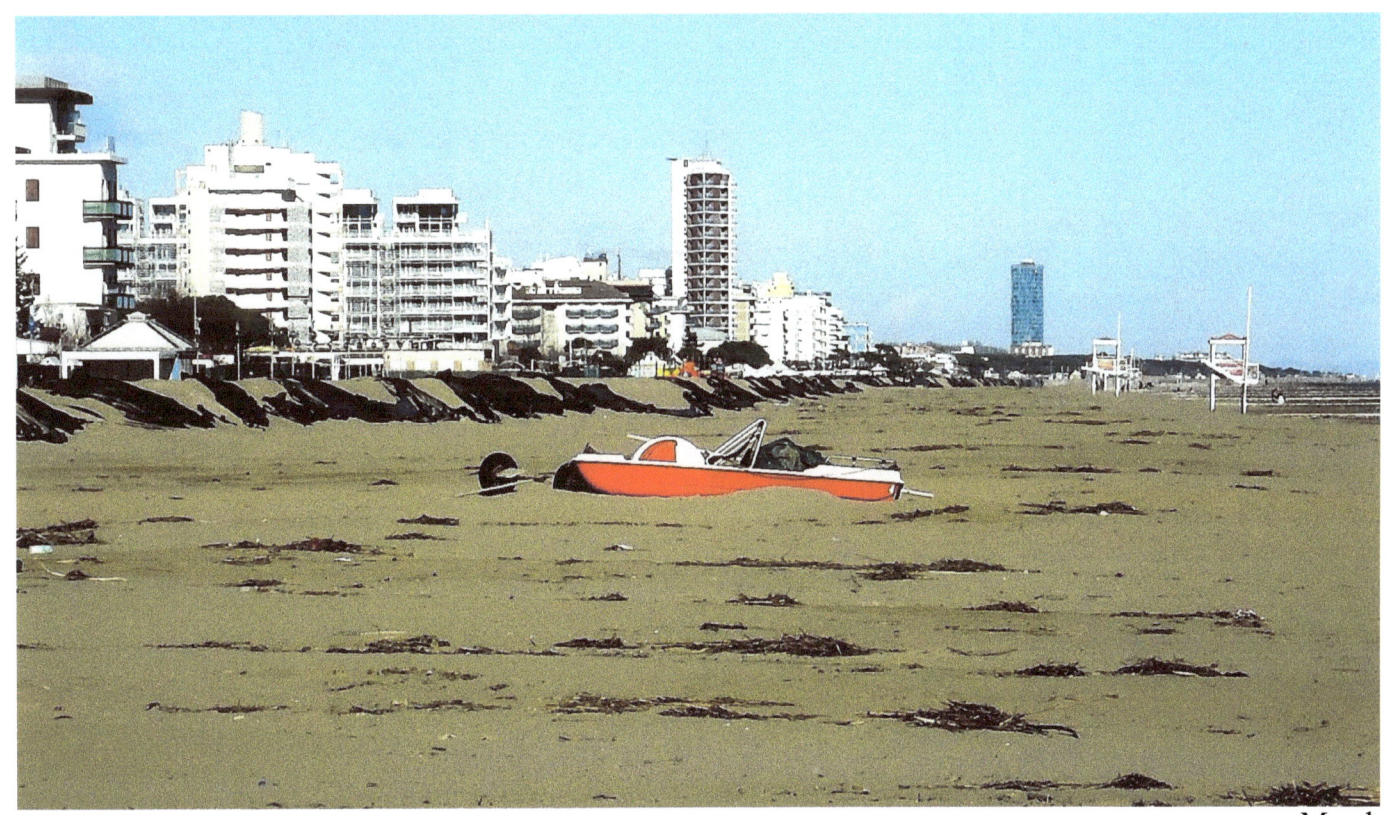
March

Capesante al forno, *scallops in the oven*. Wash the scallops well after removing the mollusc which you will wash very carefully. On each scallop put a little oil, the mollusc and the parsley with the minced garlic. Sprinkle with plenty of breadcrumbs and grated parmesan. Put in a hot oven for 15 minutes. Season with salt and serve hot.

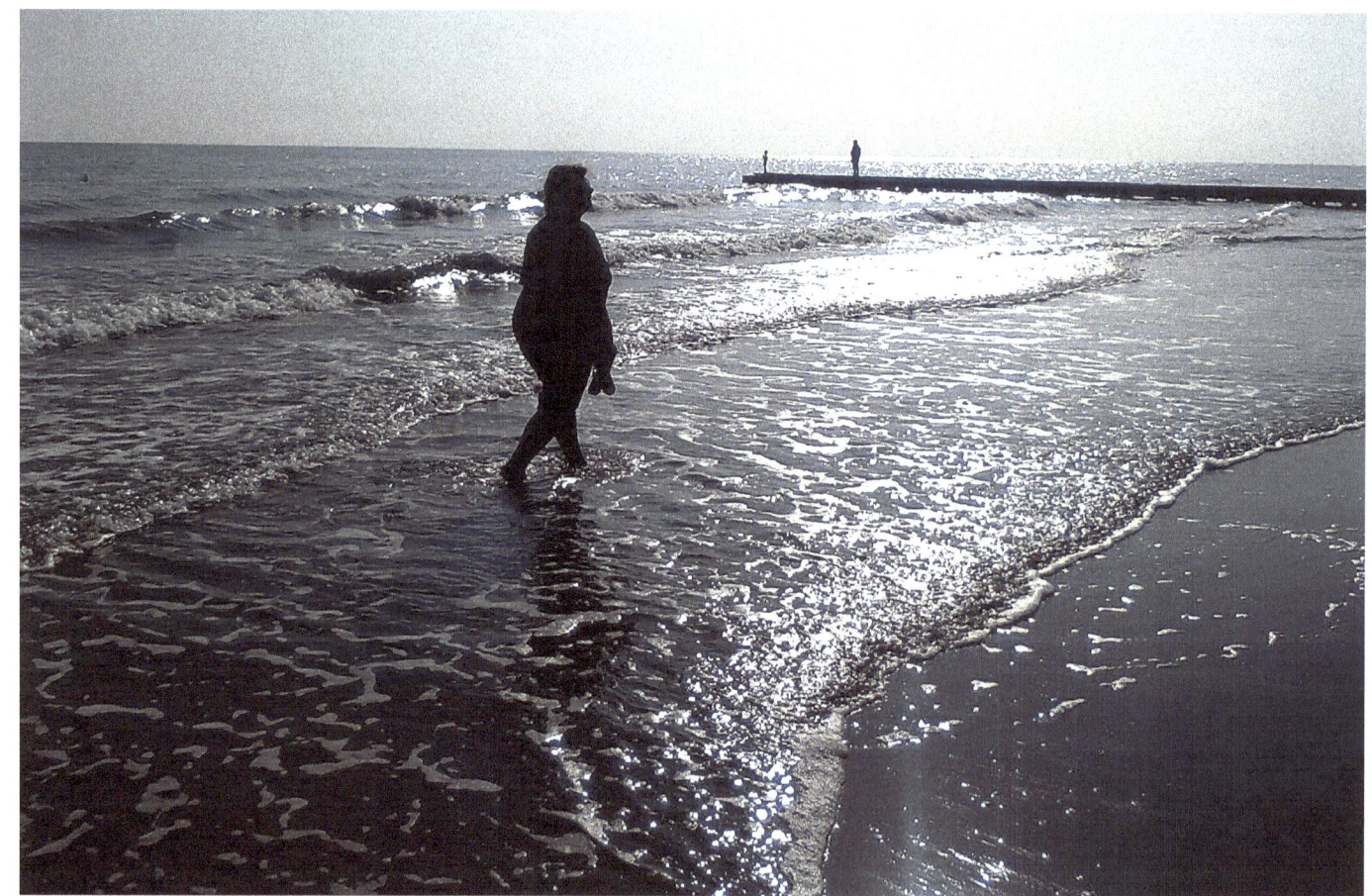
March

Masenete, *Venetian crabs*. Put a quantity to taste of masenete (crab females) in salted boiling water still alive and a little vinegar for at least ten minutes. Remove from the water and remove all the claws, remove the abdomen from the carapace and place everything in a bowl with oil, salt, pepper, garlic and parsley. The edible parts are the belly and the coral, the orange pulp inside the carapace, to be consumed preferably the day after, when they have absorbed all the taste of pesto.

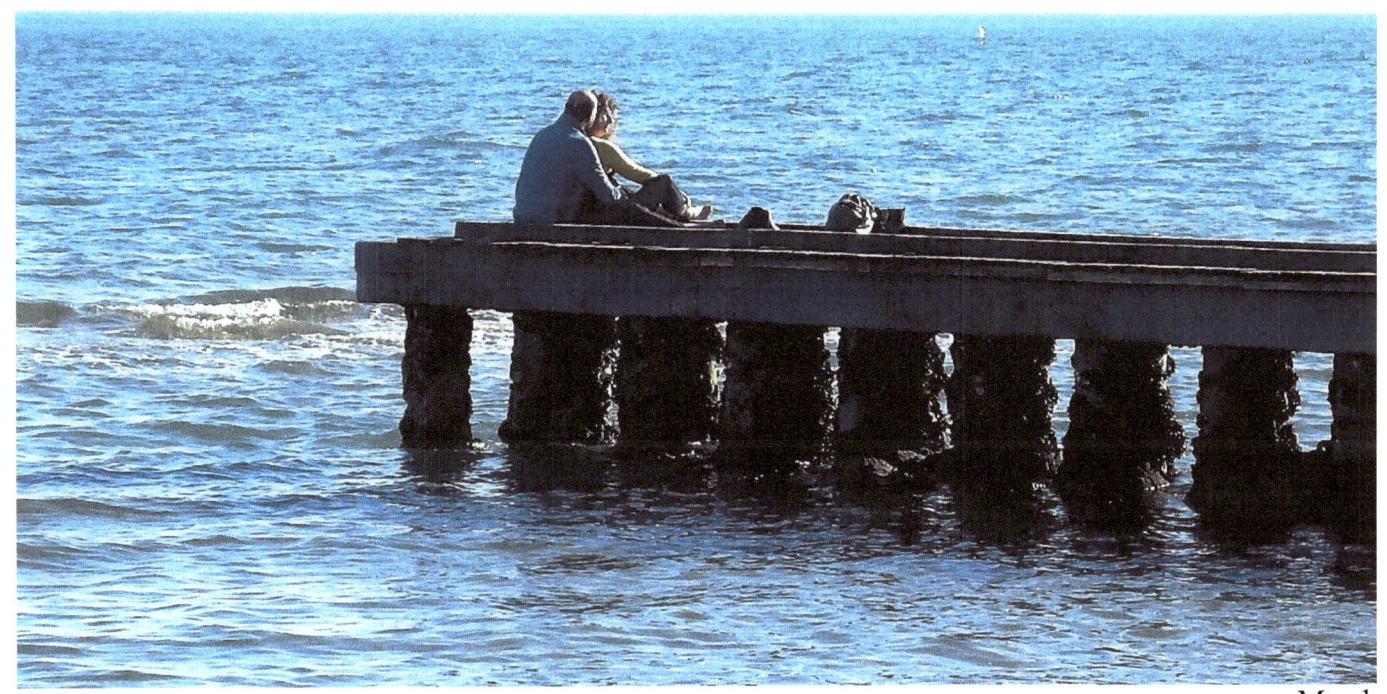

March

Peoci coe vongoe, *mussels with clams*. Purge the clams in cold water for a whole night. Brown with garlic (which must be removed later), oil and onion cut into thin slices in a large pan. Clean the mussels well and rinse the clams. Put everything in a pot, pour a little Prosecco, sprinkle the ground pepper at the time and cook covered for 15 minutes. If you want you can consume the cooking broth diping breadsticks, dry bread or more.

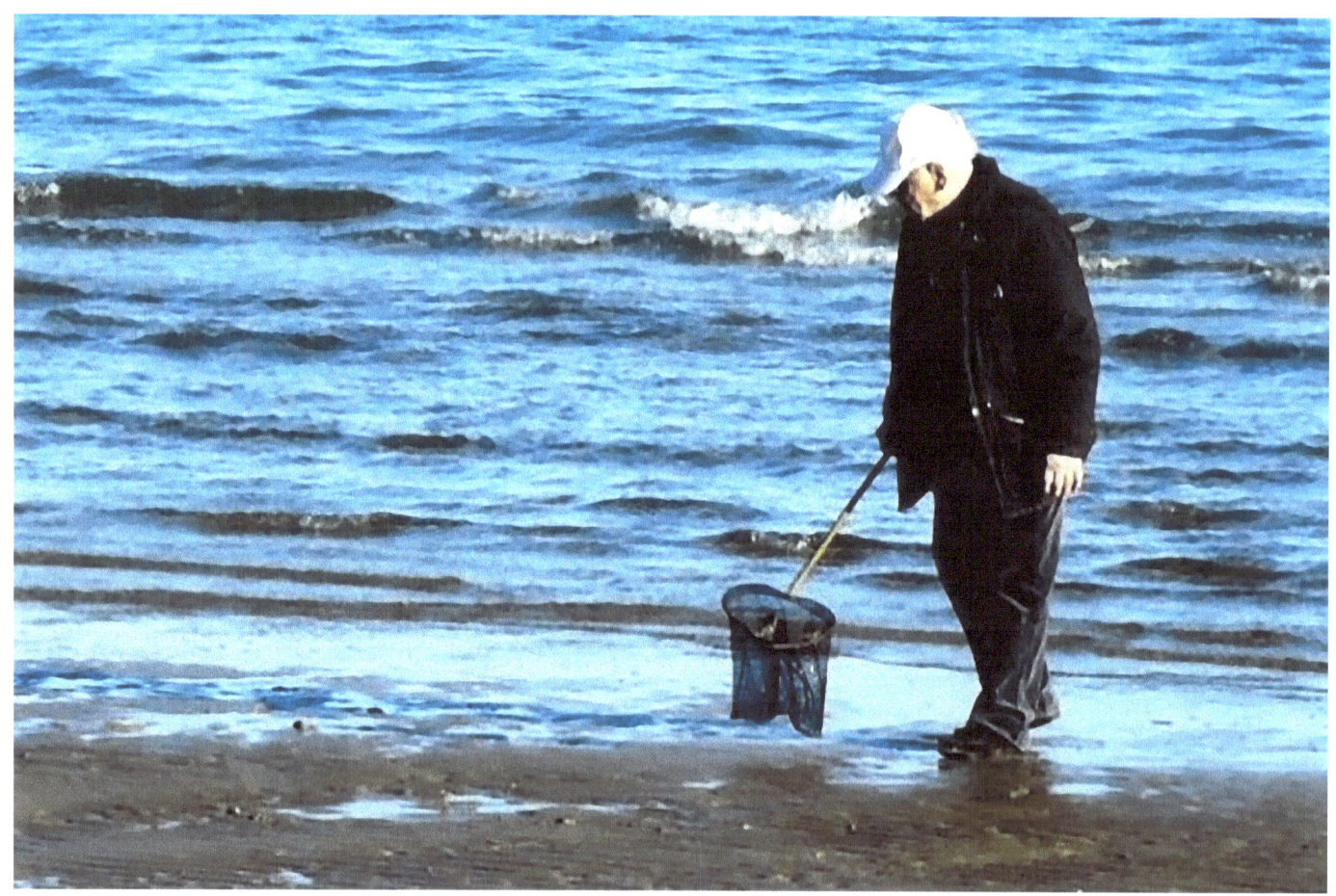

March

Pesse finto, *mock fish*. Boil the potatoes and mash them. Drain the oil from the tuna in oil and blend the tuna with anchovy fillets, gherkins and parsley. Put everything with potatoes, add mayonnaise and mix well. Season with salt and pepper. Pour the mixture into a longilineal plate and knead it until it is shaped like a fish. For an eye put an olive and with other imaginations designe the mouth, scales and fins. Cook in the oven for two or three hours.

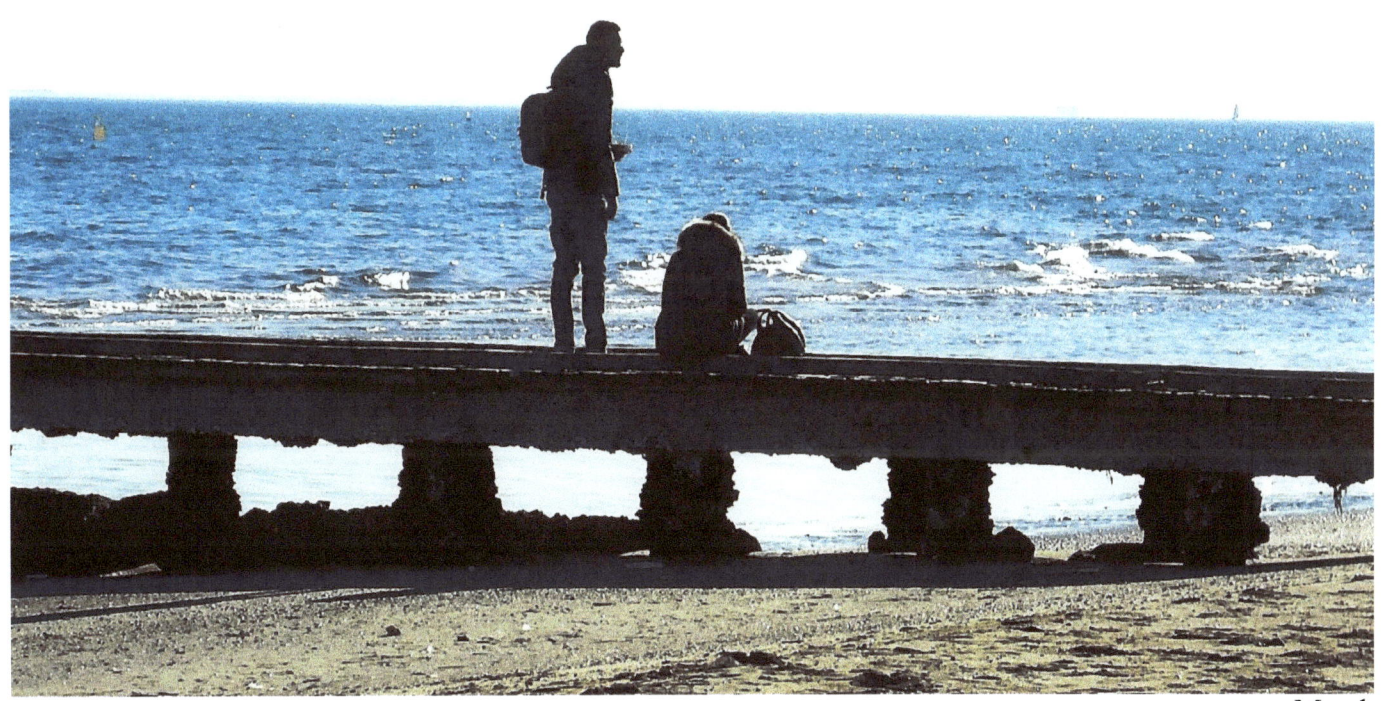
March

Sardèe a scotadèo, *sardines scottadito*. Remove the head, the fishbones and the entrails of about thirty fresh sardines. Wash them well and let drain. In a bowl prepare a freshly moist mixture of breadcrumbs, garlic powder, ground pepper and oil without exaggerating. Wrap the sardines, place them side by side in an oven dish and bake at 180 degrees for about six minutes.

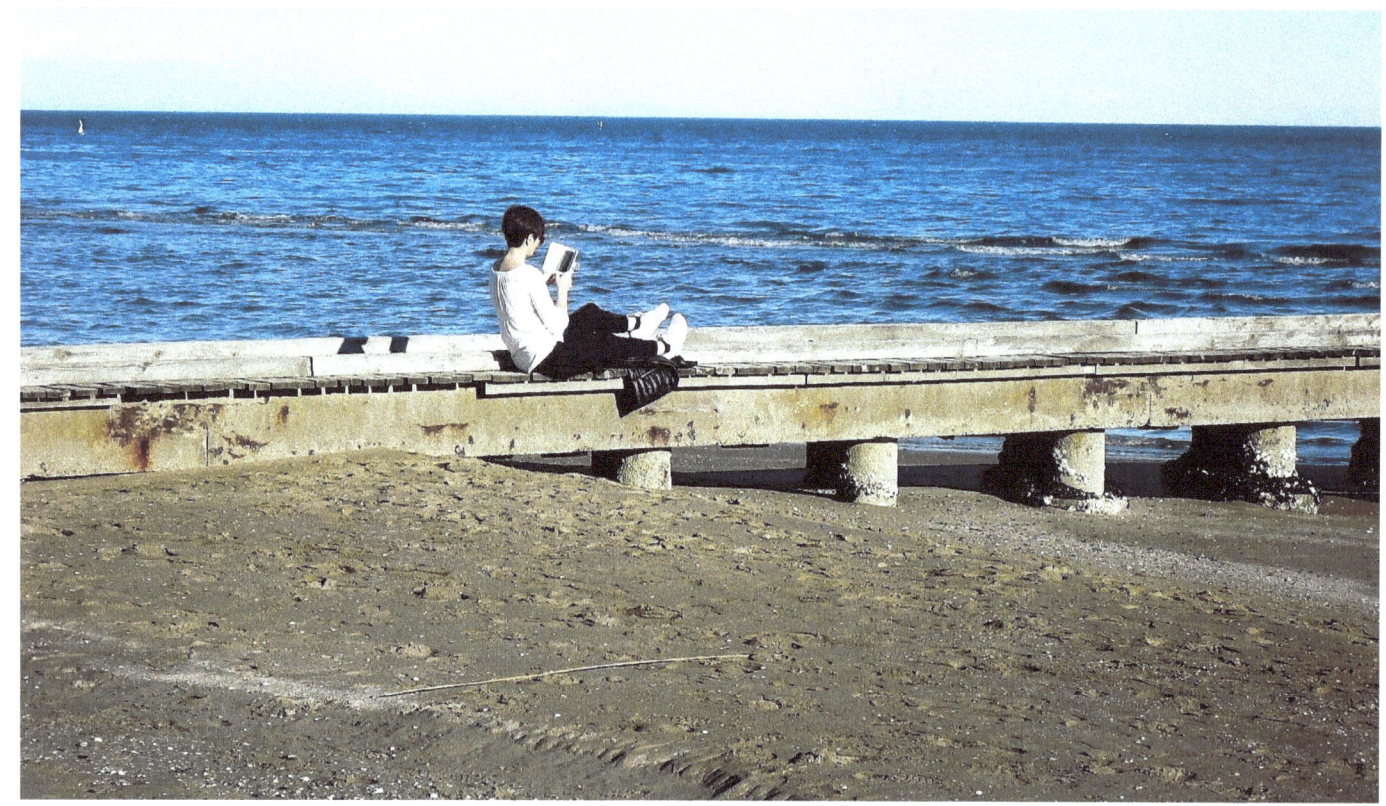

March

Sardèe in saor, *flavoured sardines*. Clean the sardines by removing the head and bowels. Wash them under running water trying to eliminate even the scales and let drip. Pass them in the flour and fry in plenty of boiling oil. Remove them from the oil and put them on the absorbent paper to remove the excess oil and salt them. When they are cooled, lay them one on top of each other in a bowl and set aside. Fry the onions (the double weight of sardines) cut into thin slices in hot oil, stirring often. As soon as they start to veil, add salt, sugar and plenty of vinegar. Continue cooking over high heat and add the raisins previously revived in hot water and pine nuts. Cover all the sardines in the bowl with the marinated onions and let them cool completely. Sardines flavoured must be consumed at least the day after.

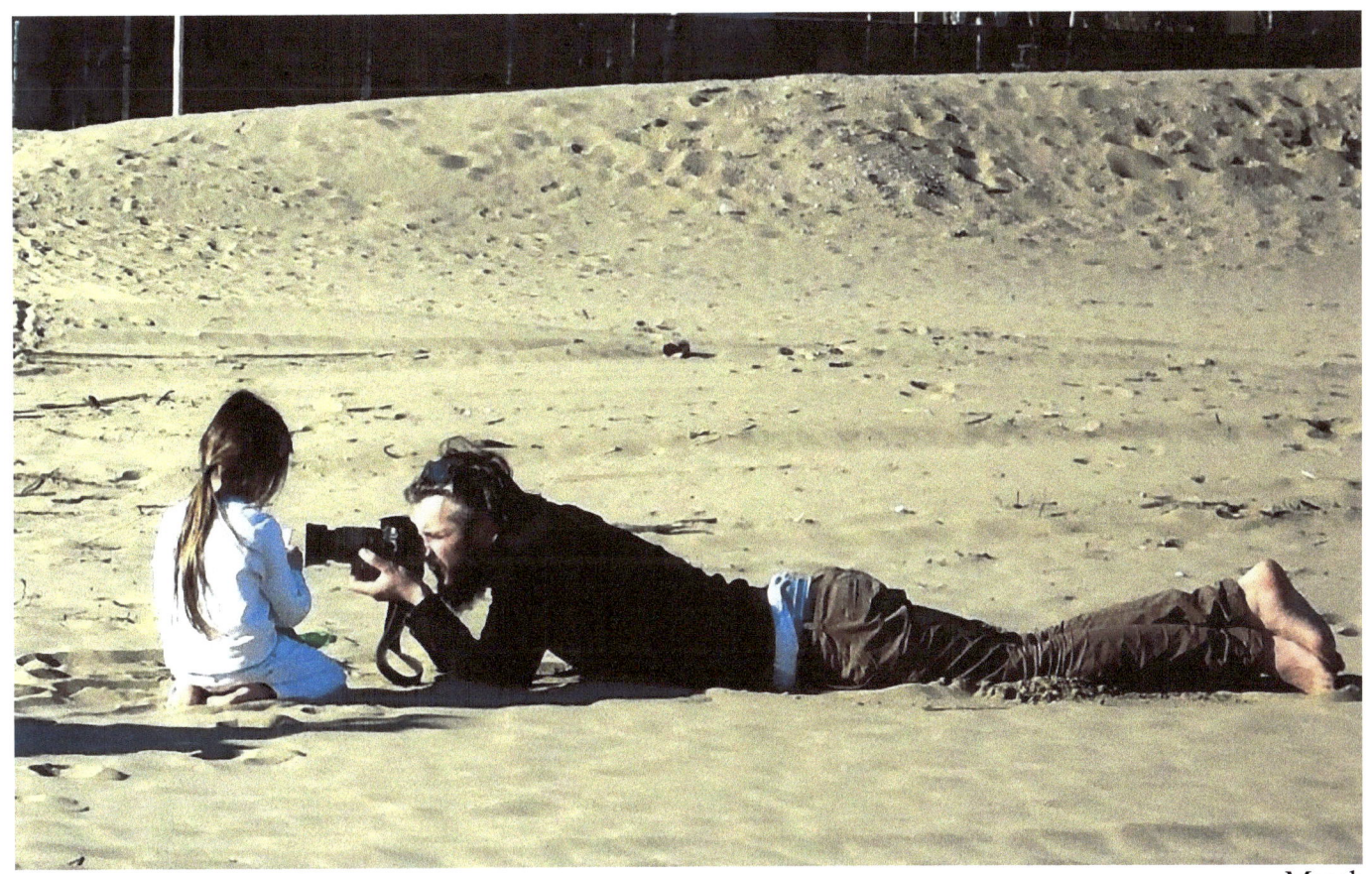

March

Schie agio e ogio, *garlic and oil shrimp*. Wash the prawns carefully under running water and then pour them into boiling salted water, adding the juice of half a lemon. As soon as a light froth rises, drain them, peel them with patience and season with an emulsion prepared with oil, garlic, minced parsley and salt. Serve with a soft polenta and fresh white wine.

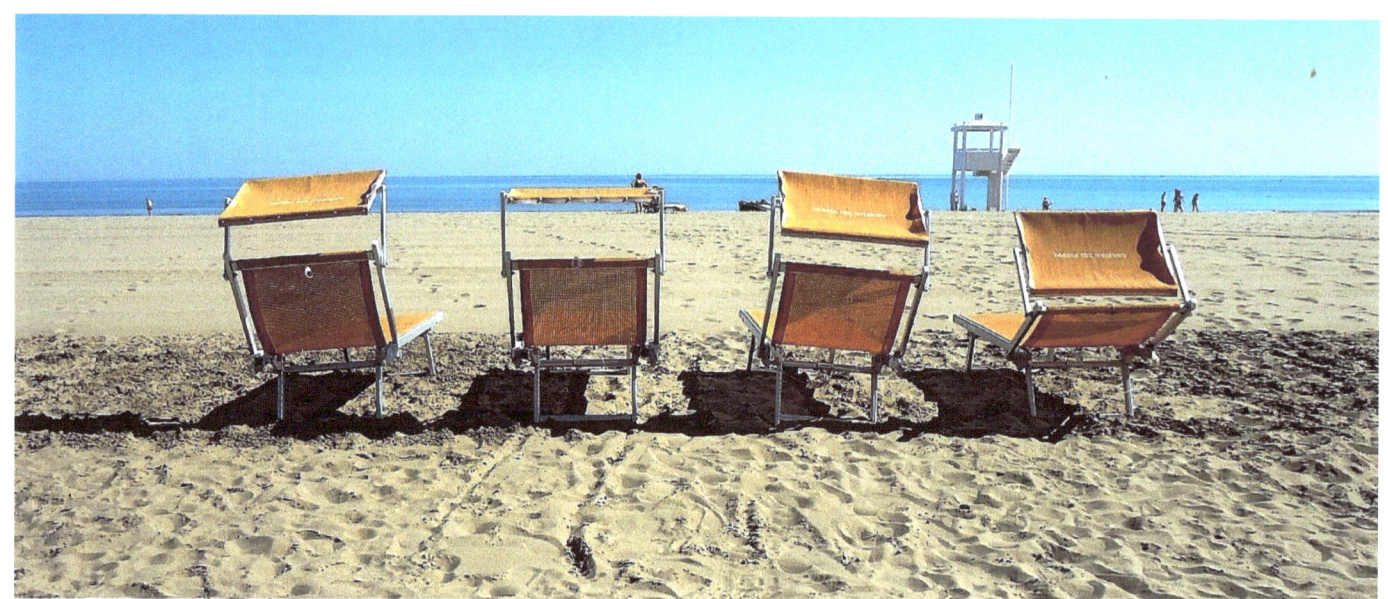
April

Bigoi in salsa, *spaghetti with sardines (or anchovies)*. In a large skillet fry the oil with the finely chopped onion, which should just soften, but not fry: for this purpose, dampen the soffritto with a little white or red wine. Add the salted sardines cut into small pieces and leave them on the fire to a minimum until they melt, but they do not have to fry. Meanwhile, boil the spaghetti and once al dente drain them and pour into the pan, stirring for two minutes over medium heat.

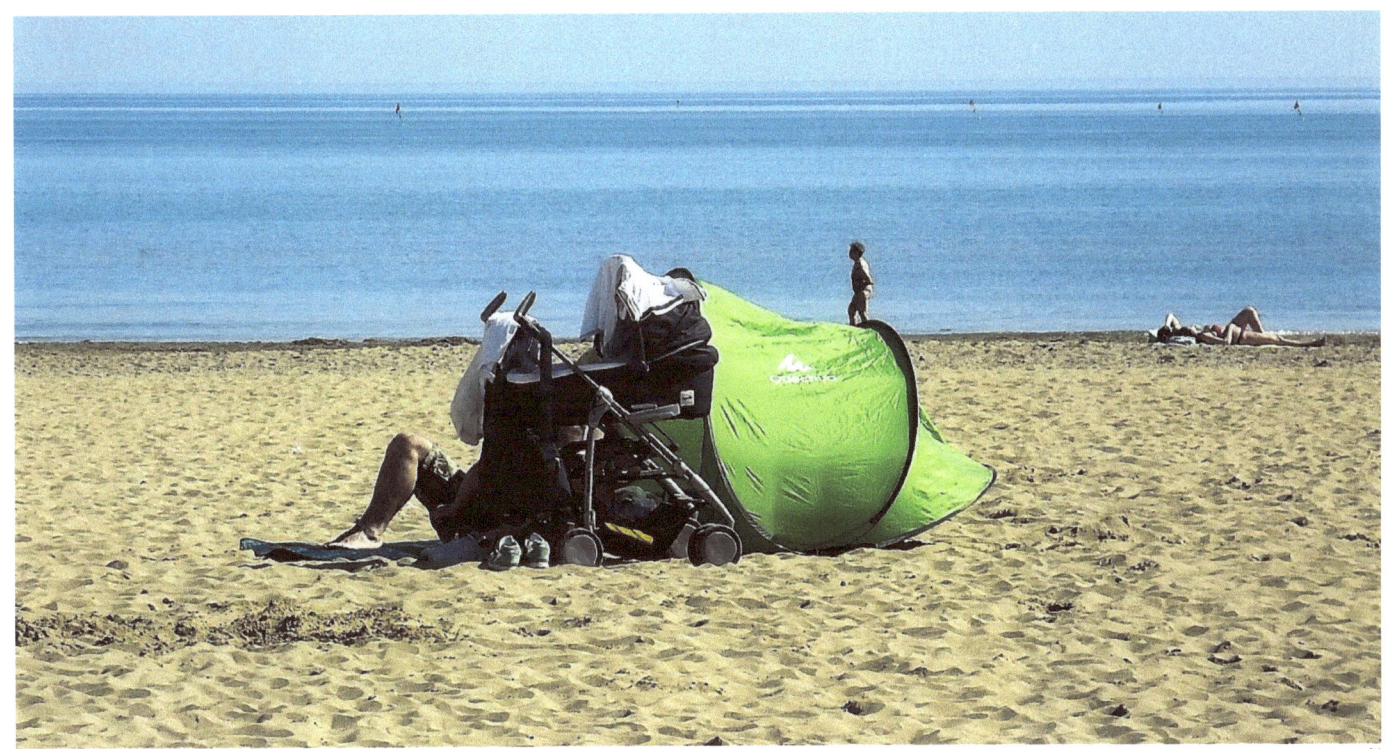

April

Rigatoni con pesce, *rigatoni with fish*. Brown in oil an onion and four cloves of garlic (to be removed immediately) in a large pan. Clean the mussels and add them to the soffritto, then put a quantity of clams of your choice, well purged previously. Cut the squid and cuttlefish into thin slices and put them in the pan with the prawns and the queen scallops, all carefully purged. Remove the tail of the prawns, cut the stomach lengthwise and put everything in the pan. After a few minutes of cooking over medium heat add the peeled tomatoes, the white wine and a teaspoon of vinegar. Adjust salt if necessary. Finally remove the stomachs of the prawns, squeeze them well and throw away. In about twenty minutes of cooking the preparation should be ready. Boil the rigatoni a little al dente and pour in a pan with the soffritto of fish to cook for another minute. Serve without adding any type of grated cheese.

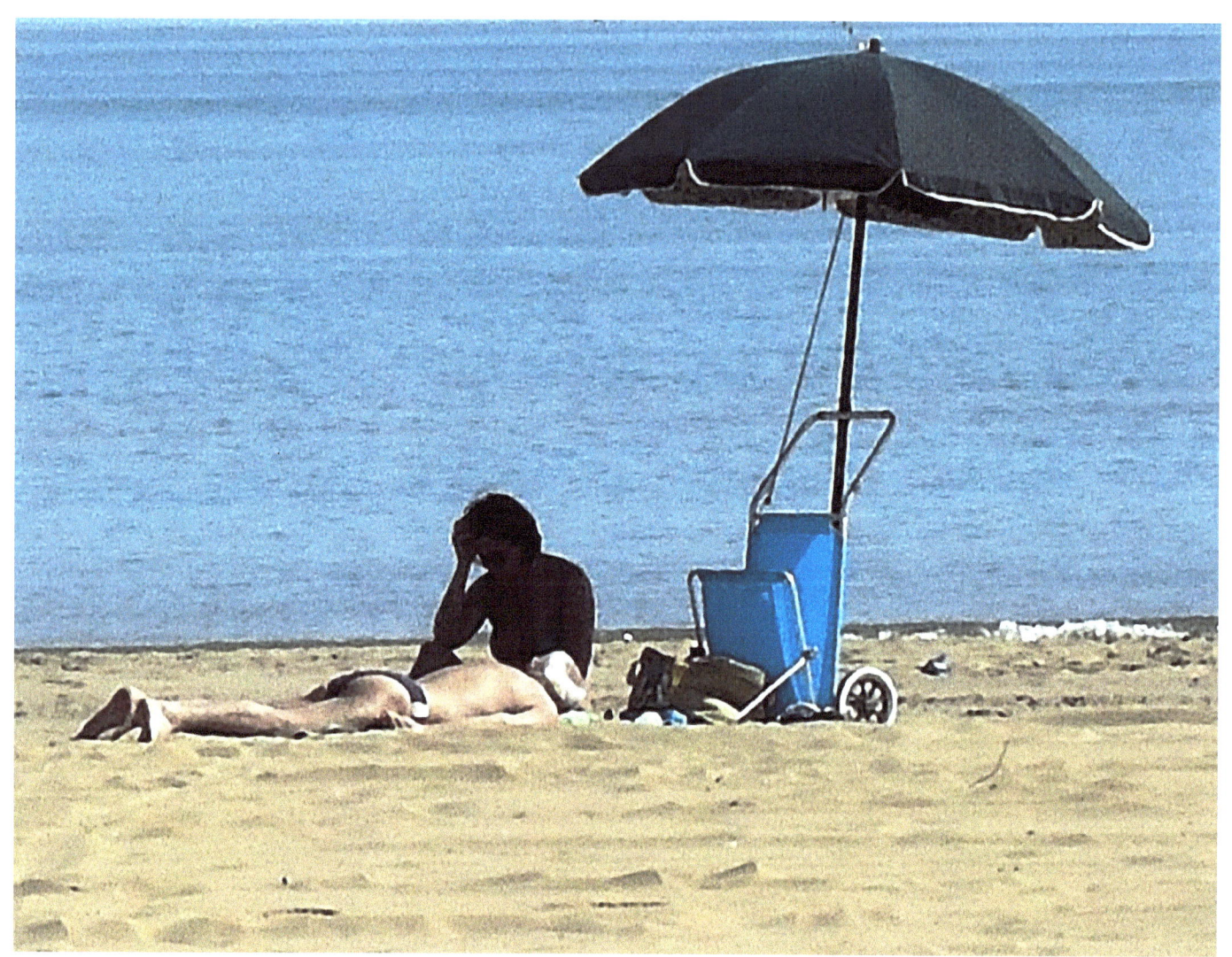

April

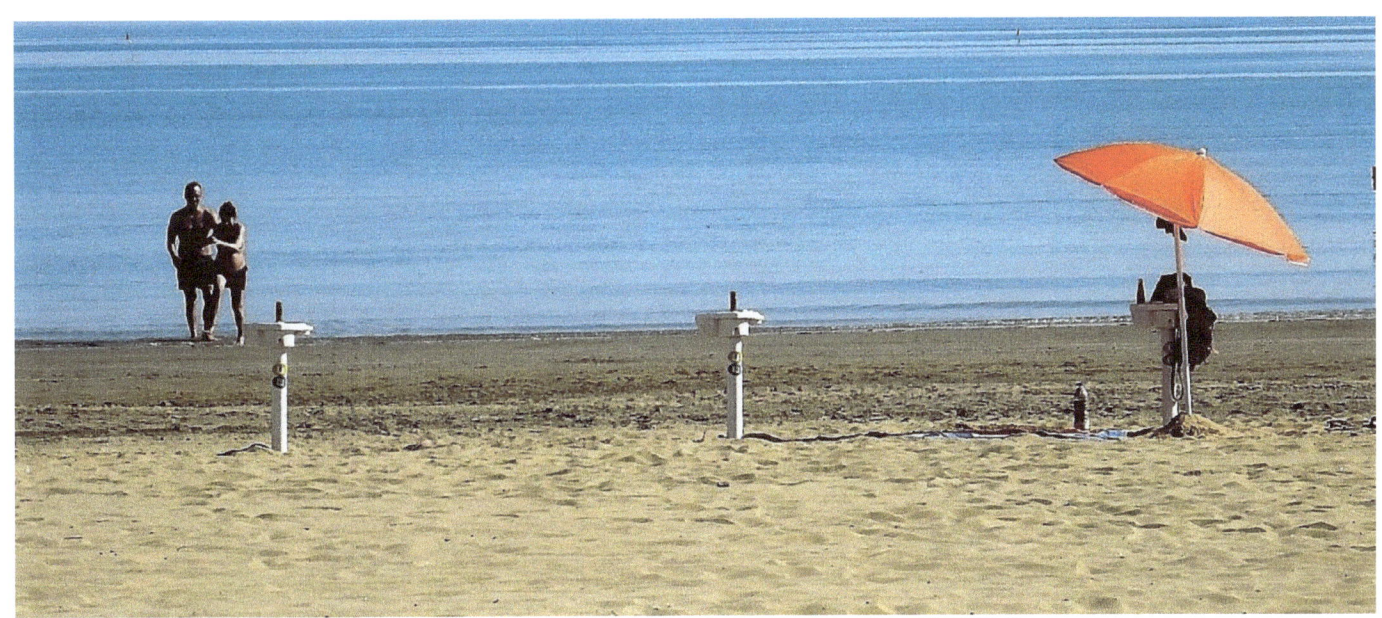
April

Risoto coi gamberoni, *risotto with prawns*. Clean the prawn tails removing the shell and the black fillet. Make a soffritto with oil, onion and garlic cloves. Put the prawns and brown for a couple of minutes. Pour a little white wine and let it evaporate. Finally add the peeled tomatoes and cook for about 10 minutes. Prepare a sauté with onion and butter, add the rice and fry for 2 minutes, stirring constantly. Dissolve a bag of saffron in a cup of hot stock and pour it over the rice. Continue cooking as for a normal risotto for about twenty minutes until it is very compact. Pour the risotto onto the plate, make a hole in the center and fill it with the prawns. Sprinkle with chopped parsley and serve hot.

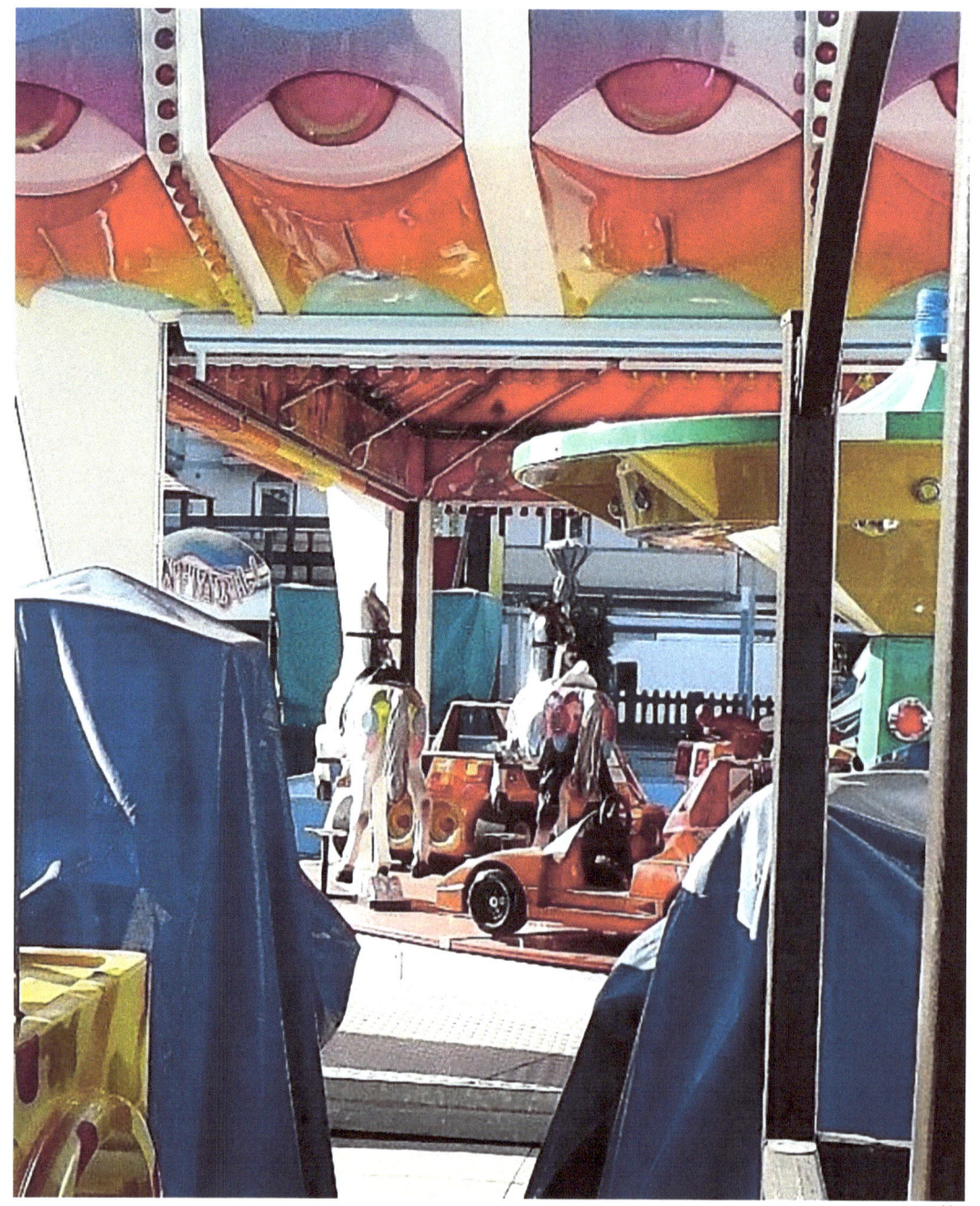

April

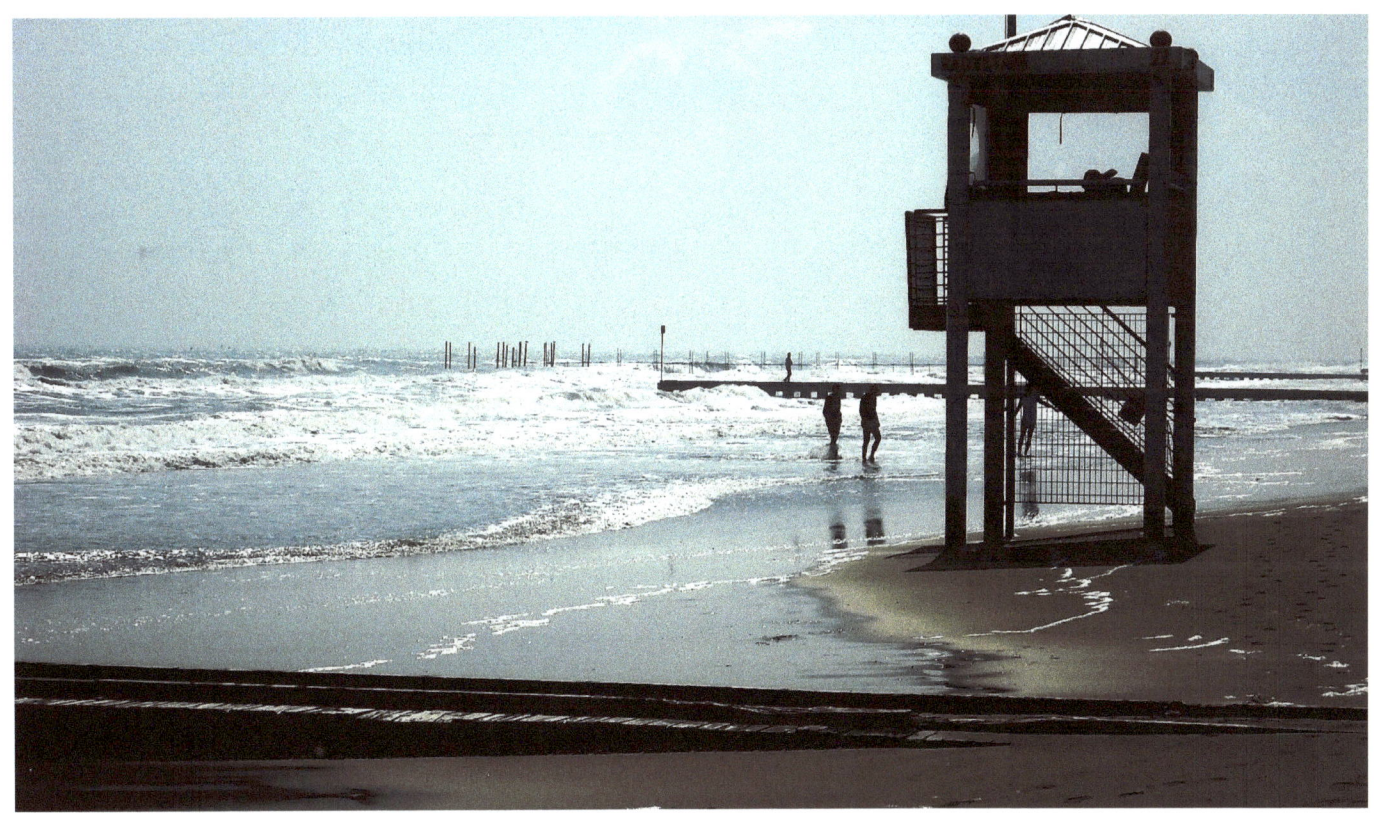
May

Risoto de canoce, *risotto of sea cicadas*. Cook the cicadas and use the broth to cook the risotto, which you will add hot on the rice a little at a time, stirring constantly with a wooden spoon. Finally put a little butter, pepper and a finely chopped garlic and parsley. If necessary, adjust salt.

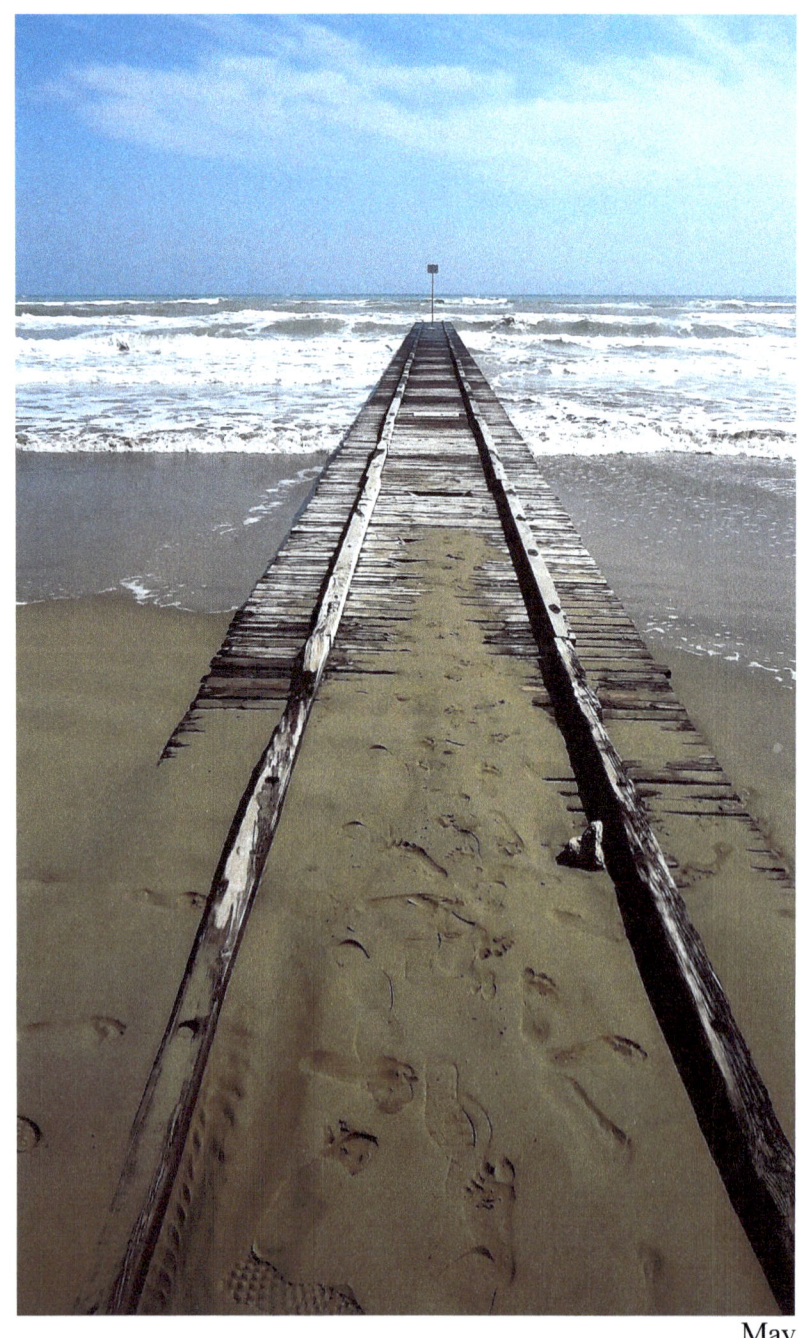

May

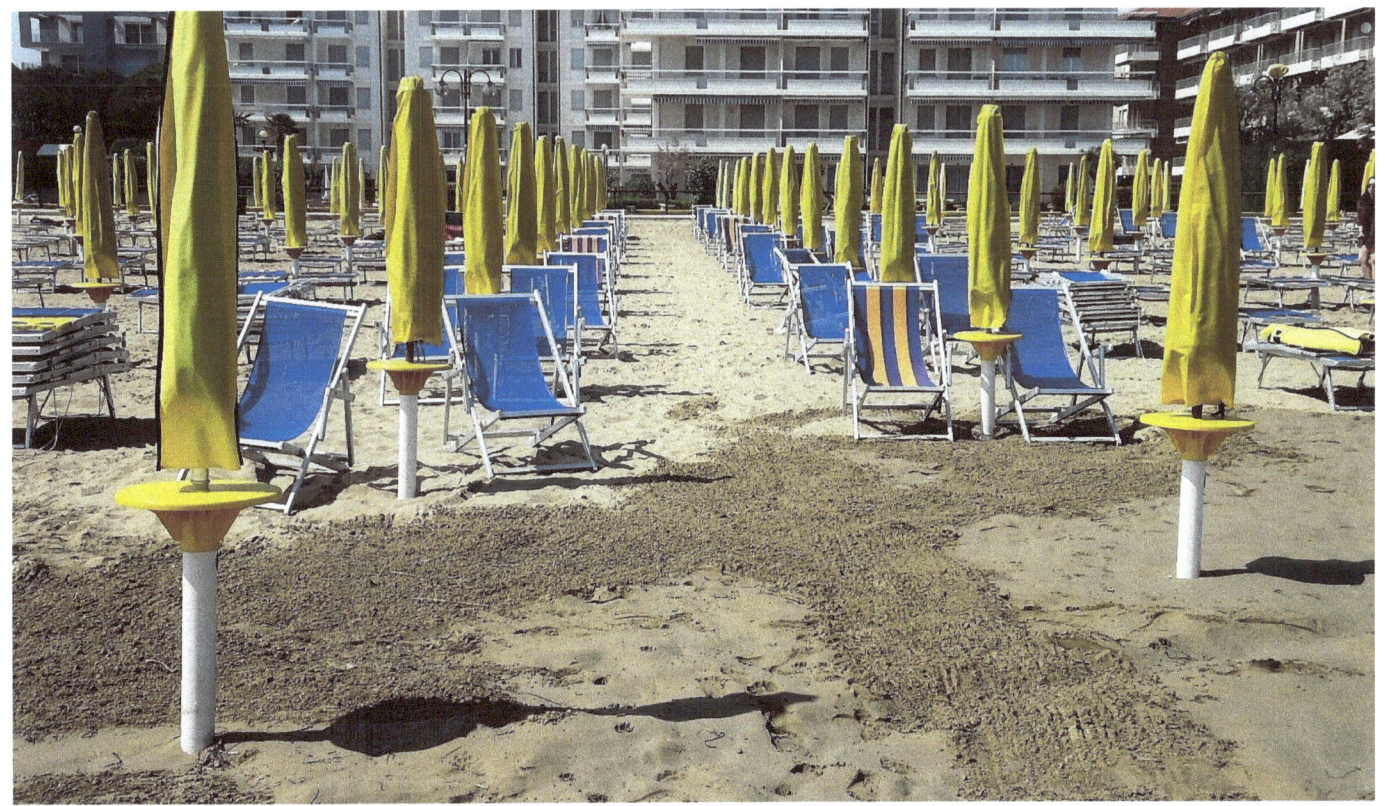
May

Baccalà mantecato, *creamed stockfish*. Wash the fresh baccalà, place it in a pot and cover with water and milk. Boil 20 minutes, then turn off the heat and let it cool in its cooking liquid. Drip it and peel it, then crumble it completely with your hands removing any fishbones. Put it in a large bowl and beat it with a wooden spoon while pouring in the oil. Continue to defibrate the pulp for at least 15 minutes until a creamy consistency is obtained. Finally add the parsley and a finely chopped garlic clove to the cod. Serve warm with white polenta croutons.

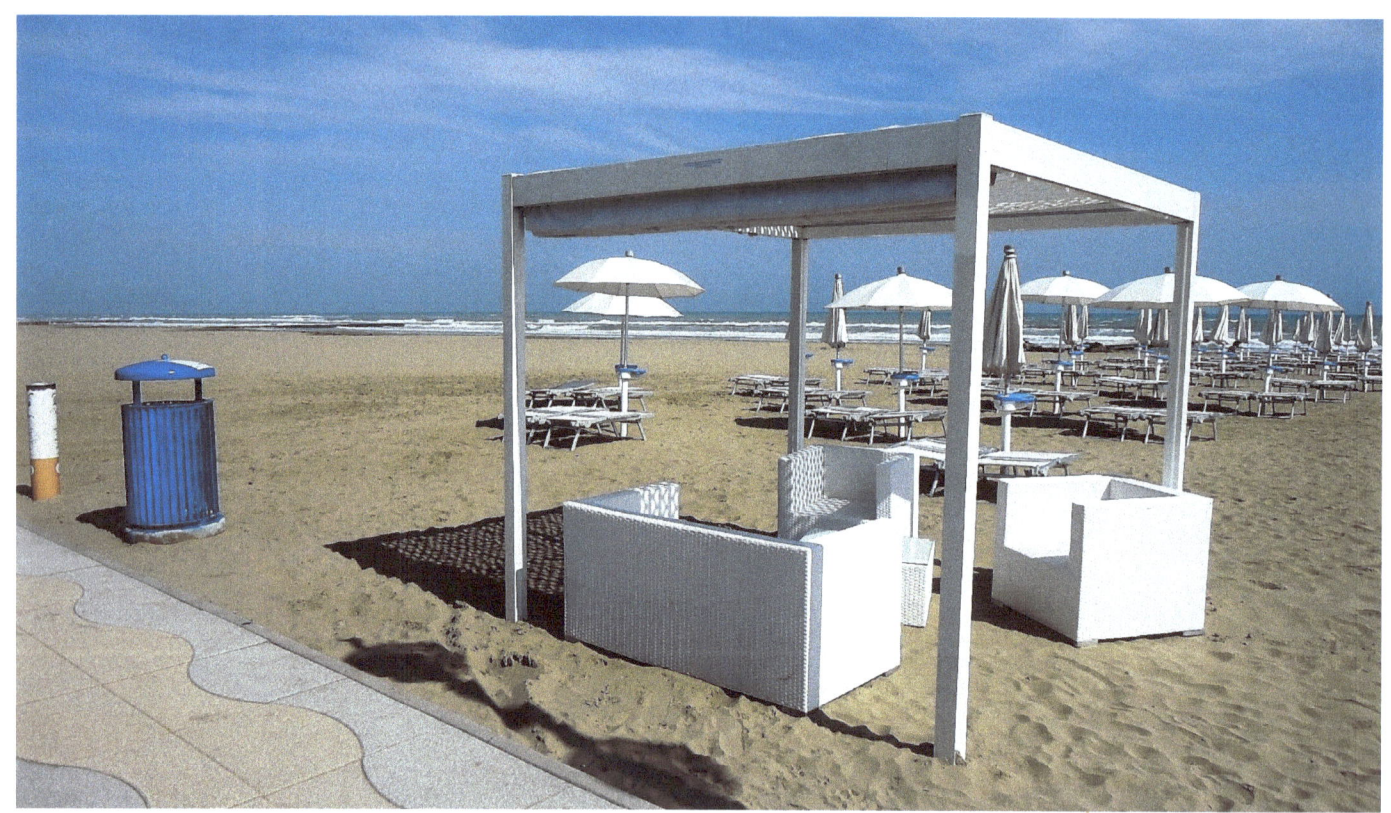

May

Bisata in tecia, *stewed eel*. Brown in oil half a thinly cut onion, two cloves of garlic, a minced carrot and celery. Remove the garlic, cut the eel into pieces and place them on the soffritto with a little white wine. Add the peeled tomatoes and cook for ten minutes, turning from time to time without breaking the pieces of eel, which should be accompanied with a tender white polenta.

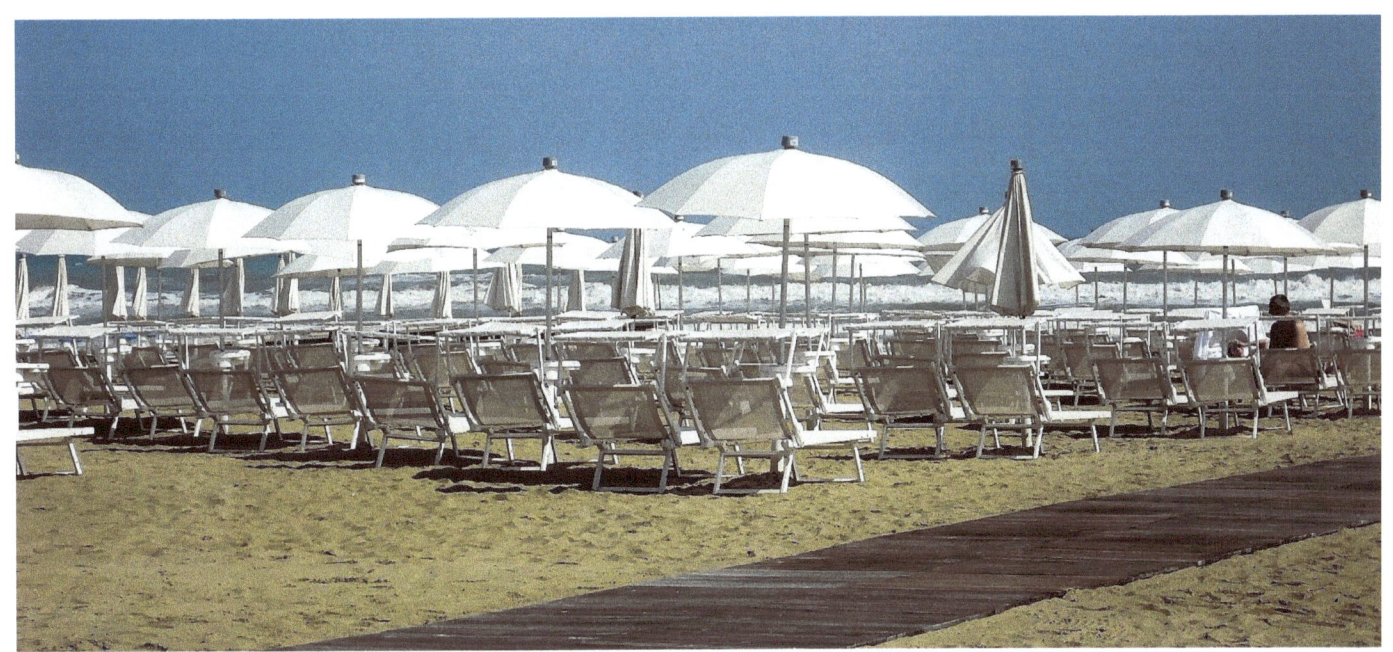

May

Bisato su l'ara, *Murano eel*. Gut and clean a large eel of lagoon and cut it on two sides with cuts a dozen centimeters apart. Place a layer of bay leaves on the bottom of a large clay pot, place the eel wrapped in a spiral, season with salt and pepper and cover with another layer of bay leaves. You do not need any other ingredients because the fish will cook in its own condiment released by very oily skin. The ideal would be to cook the large eel a slow on the burning embers, for example a barbecue, but in absence you can cook in the oven the pan and cook until the pulp becomes white. Serve accompanied by a steaming polenta and young and fresh red wine.

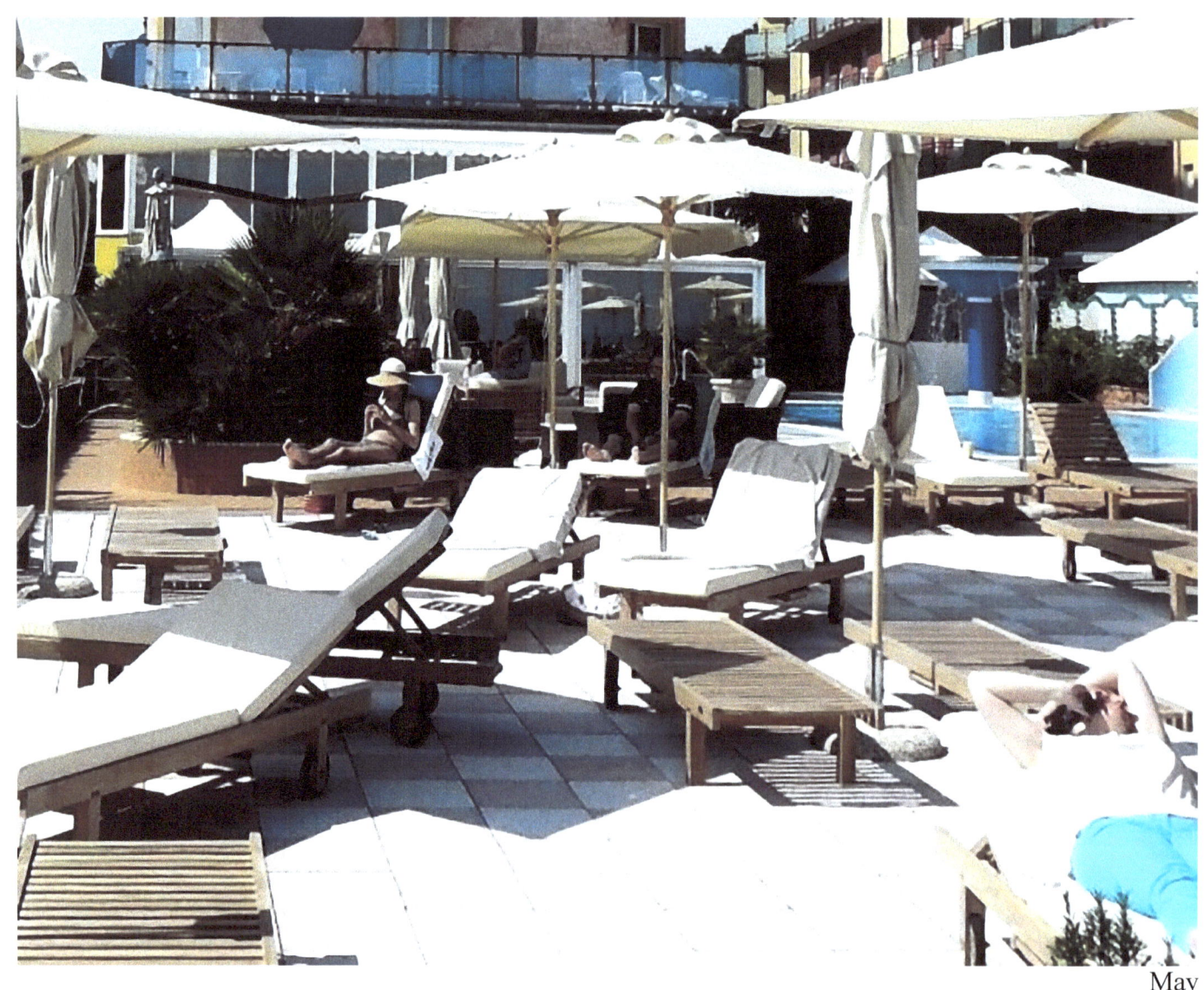

May

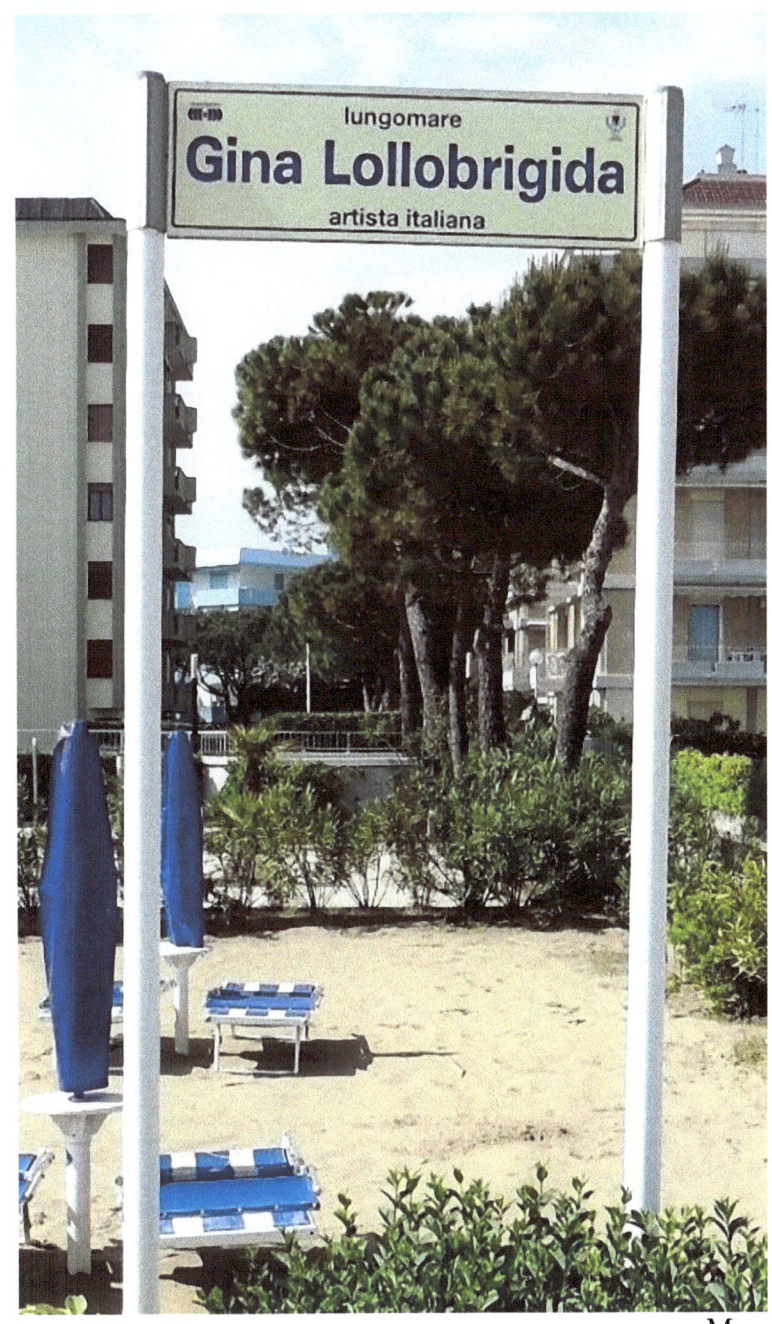

May

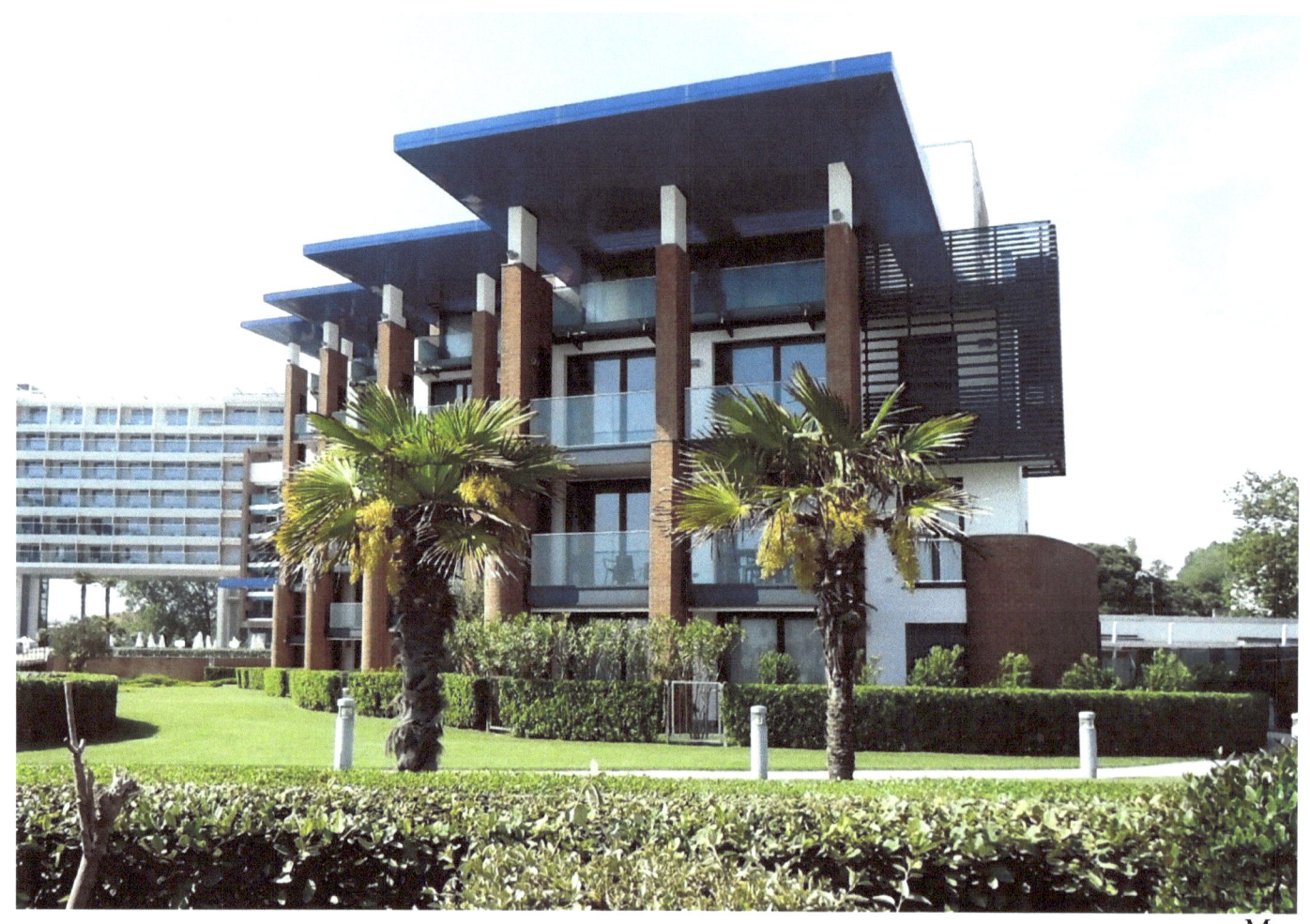
May

Branzino sotto sale, *sea bass in salt*. Clean a sea bass well and fill the belly with garlic and onion cut into thin slices. Mix three kilos (or even more) of coarse salt with a cup of flour, the aromas (rosemary, thyme, sage, etc.), the juice of a lemon and a cup of water. Spread the mixture of salt into a baking dish forming a layer of two centimeters and lay the sea bass, which you cover again with garlic and onion. In the end cover all the fish with the rest of remained salt for a layer of at least one centimeter. Cook in the oven at 180 degrees for 40 minutes. Remove from the oven, break the hardened salt, gently clean the sea bass from the remained salt and make some fillets. Serve with a drizzle of extra virgin olive oil and chopped parsley.

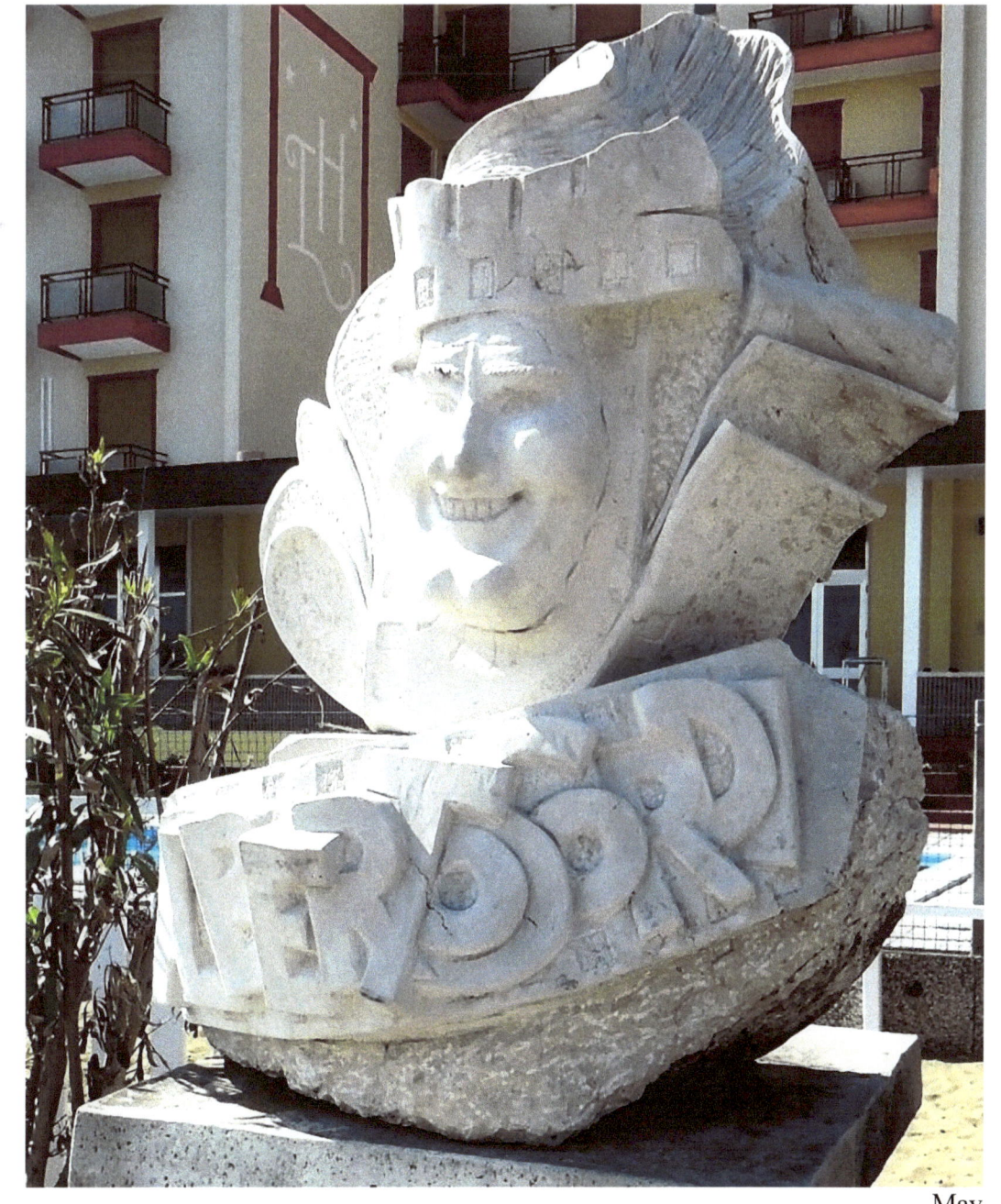

May

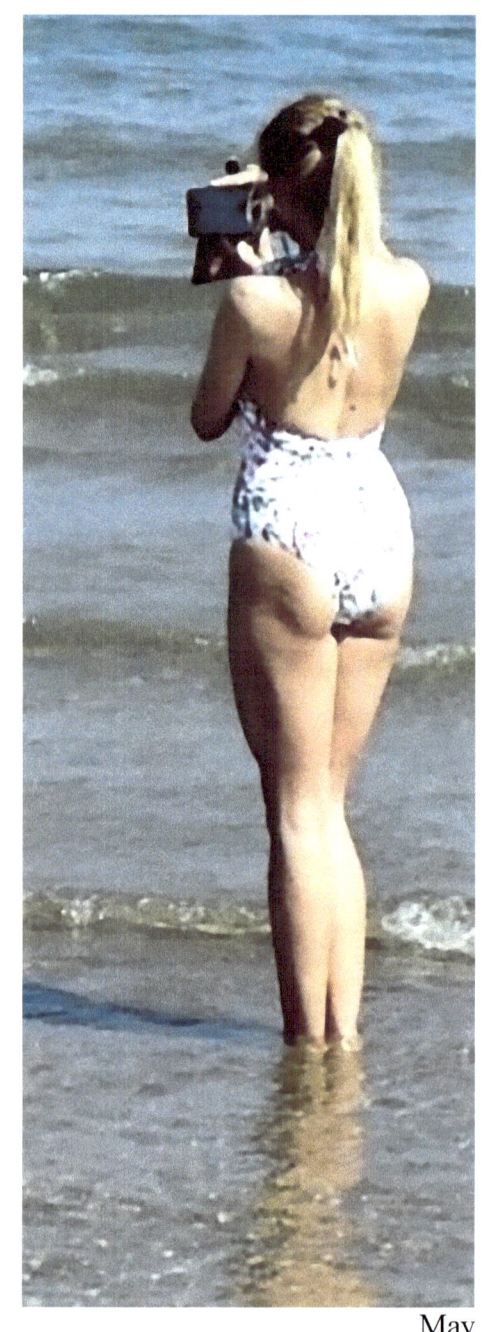

May

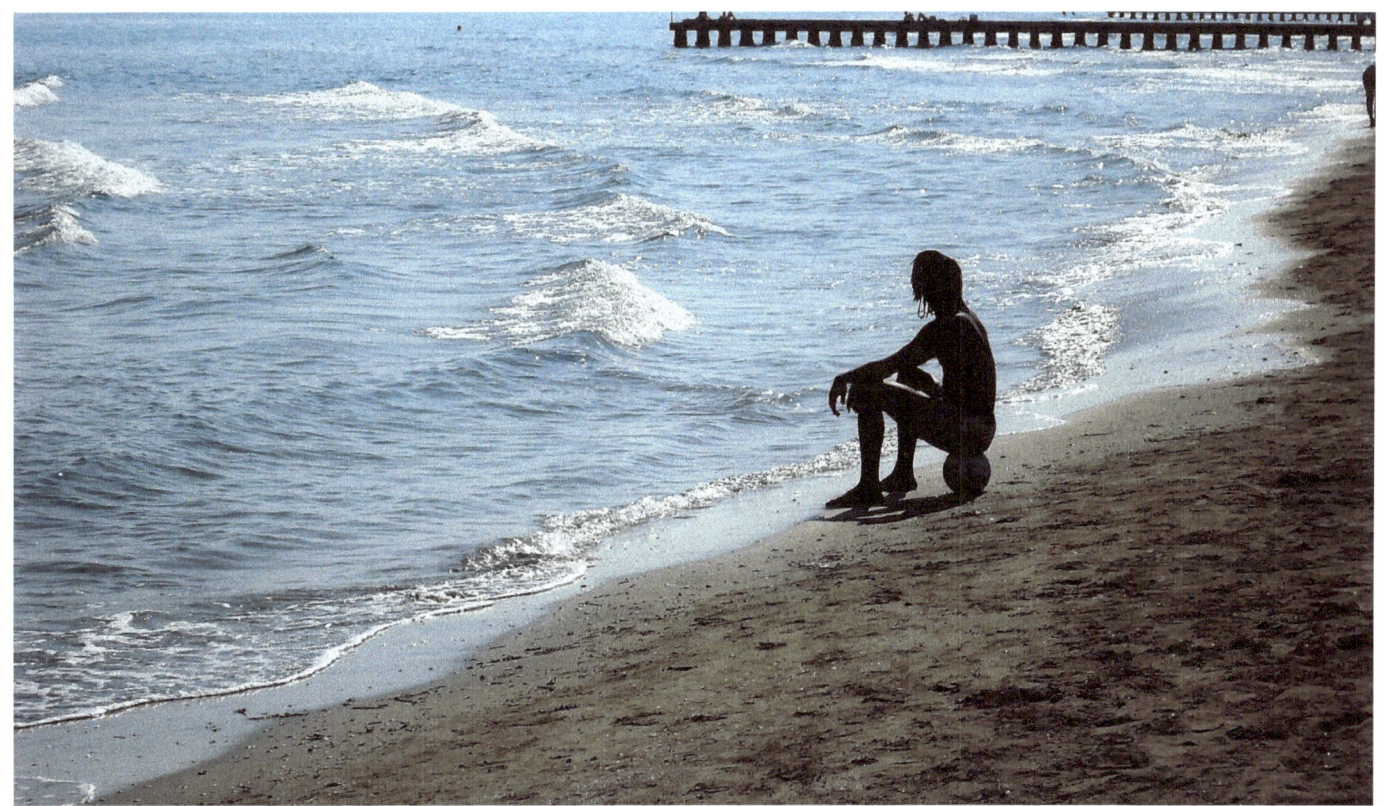
May

Cagnoéto in umido, *smooth hound (Palombo) stewed*. Fry the onion, the carrot, the celery in small pieces and a clove of garlic, which will then be removed. Cut even the fresh cagnoéto into small pieces, put it in the sauté, pour a little wine and let it brown for one minute over high heat. Add the peeled tomatoes, the basil and season with salt and pepper. Continue cooking without lid for ten minutes. Serve hot with tender polenta.

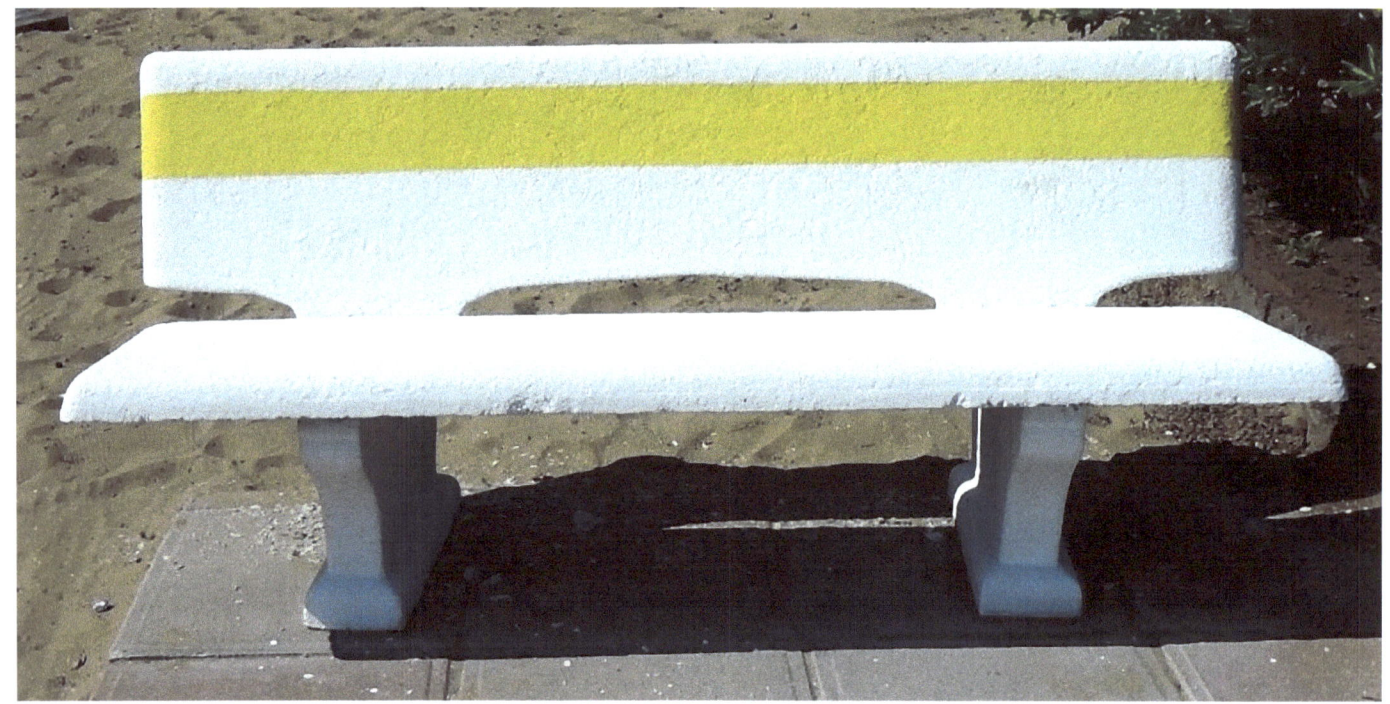
May

Calamari con carciofi, s*quid with artichokes*. Clean the fresh artichokes by removing the hard leaves and the upper part. Fry an onion in oil, put the chopped artichokes and pour white wine. Add the calamari cut into small pieces and season with salt and pepper. Wet two loaves of stale bread in the milk and let it soak, then squeeze it and make a mixture adding the fried artichokes and two whole eggs. Adjust salt. Fill with this dough a pair of squids each, put them in a pan with a little oil and bake at 180 degrees. Meanwhile, prepare a sauce with onion, abundant peeled tomatoes and fresh broad beans or pitted olives, making it dry in a pan on the fire with a little oil. Halfway through cooking, cover the calamari and leave them in the oven until completely cooked. Serve hot.

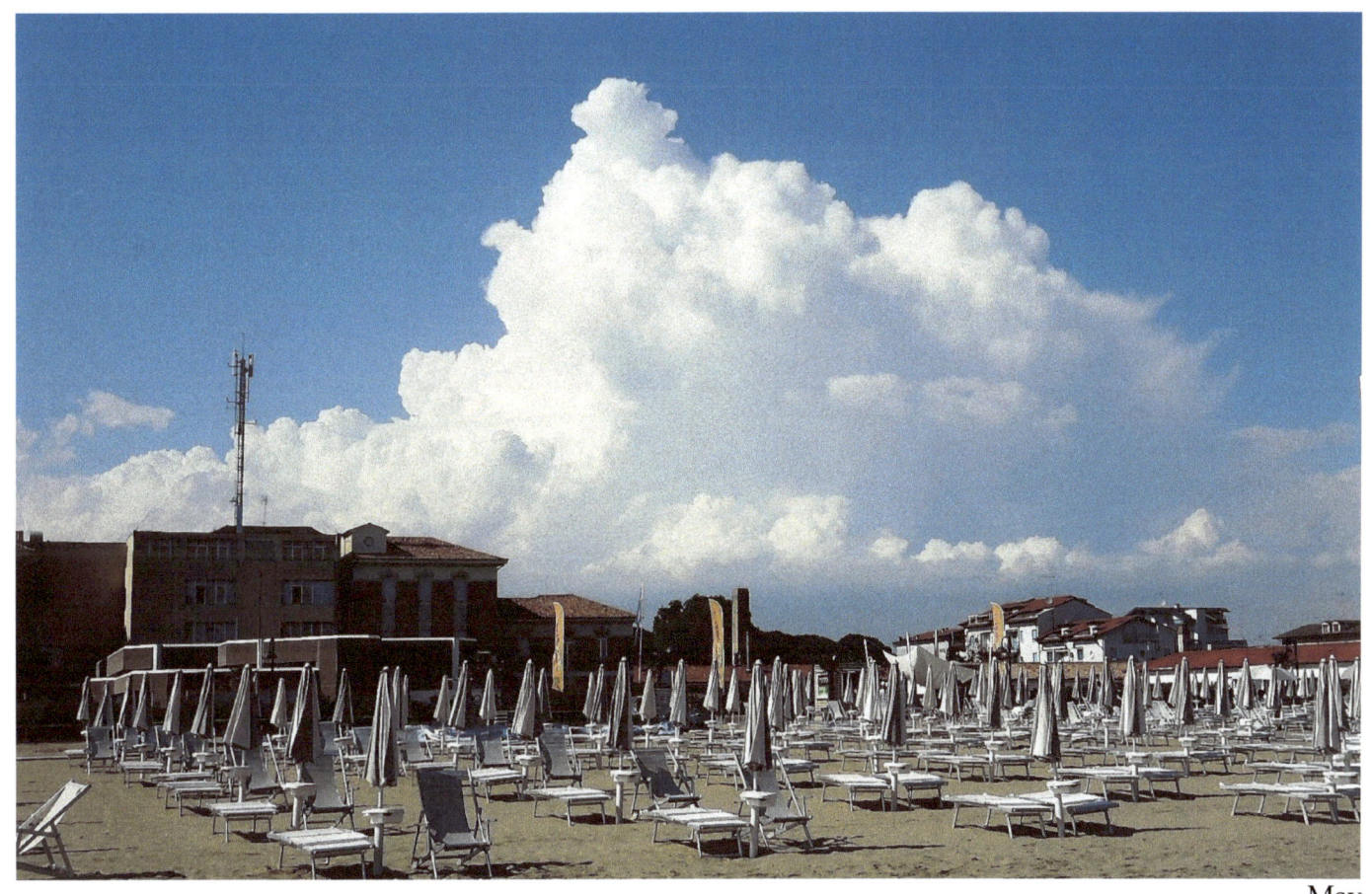

May

Frittata con i gamberi, *frittata with prawns*. Fry the prawns in a pan of oil until they are crisp. Beat the eggs in a bowl and pour them on the fried prawns. Adjust salt, mix everything well and finish cooking as for a normal frittata.

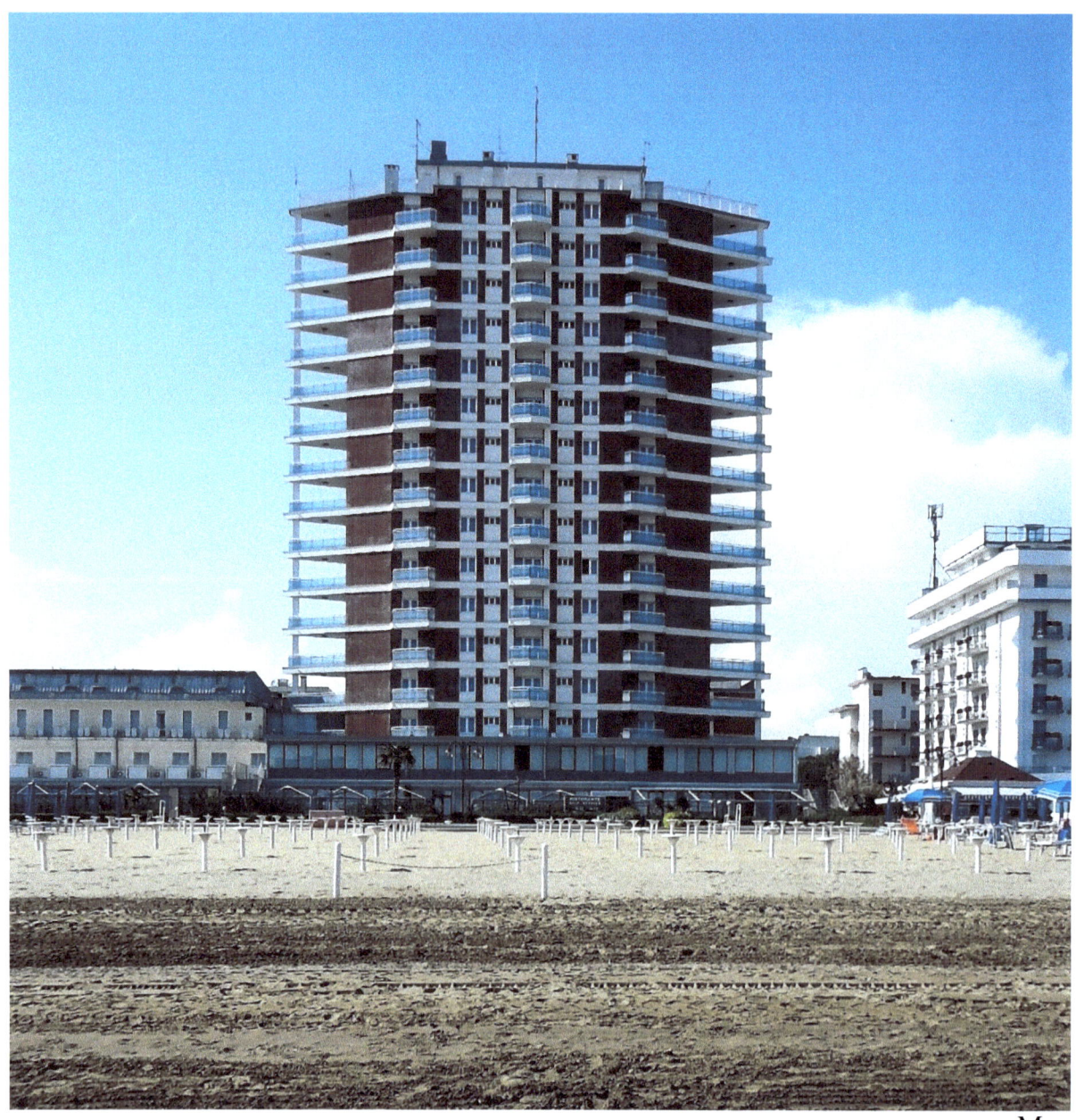

May

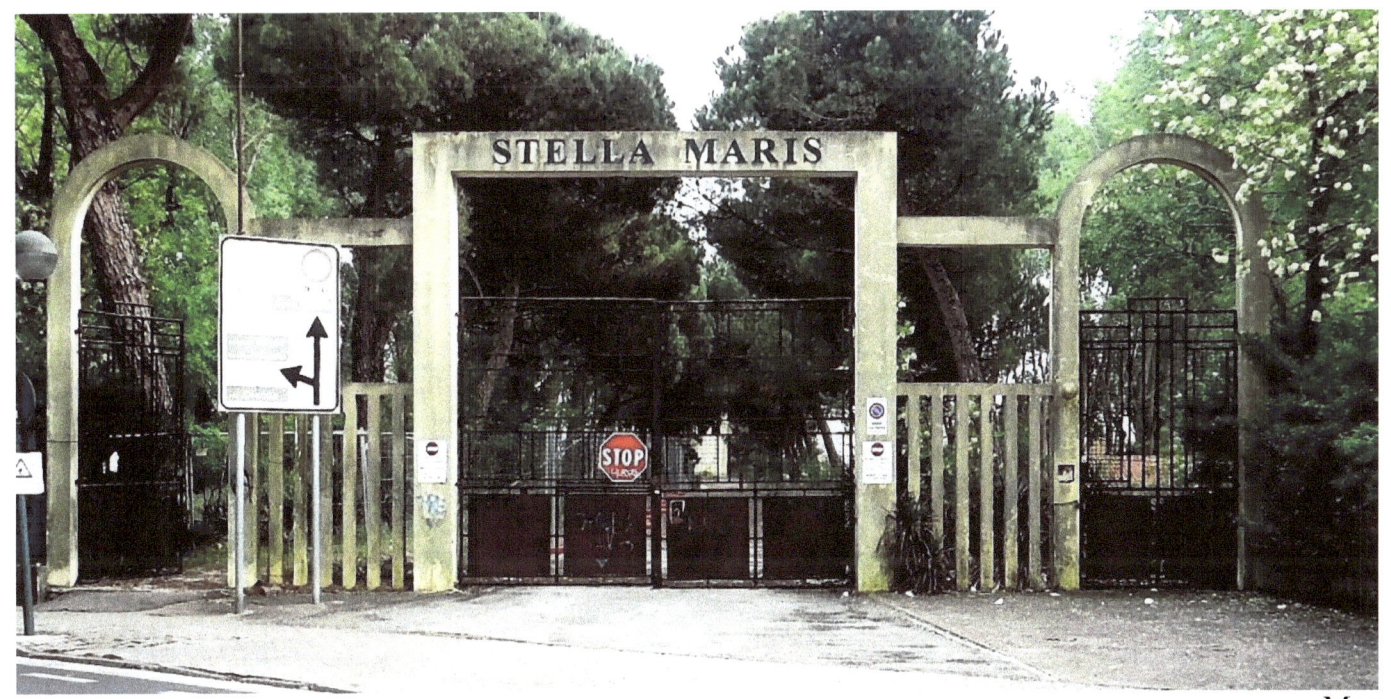

May

Moéche frite, *fried green crabs*. Wash the moéche with plenty of salted water. Cut the ends of the legs, drain well and flour them. Fry them a few minutes in hot peanut oil until they become golden and crisp. Remove and dry with absorbent paper, salt and serve with a few cloves of lemon.

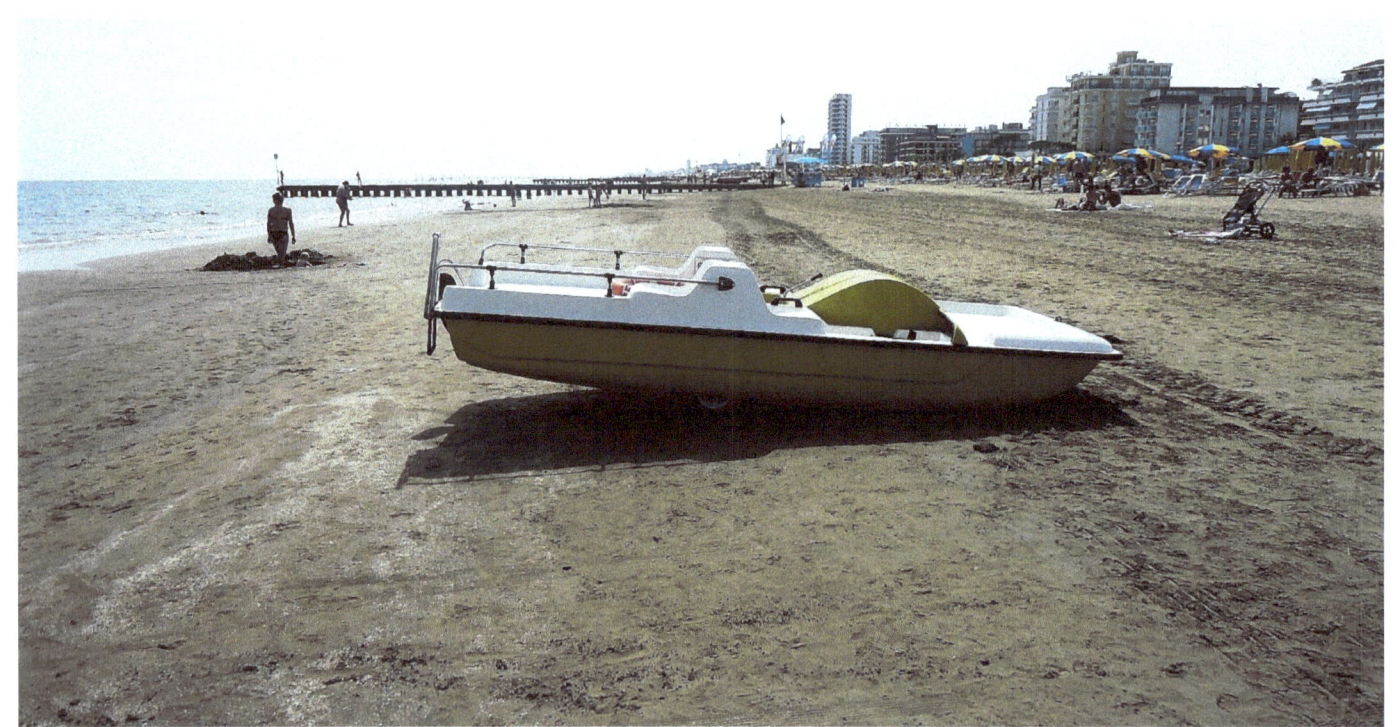

June

Insalata di piovra, *octopus salad*. Put the octopus under ice for at least 48 hours. Boil plenty of water in a large pot with onion, carrot and celery. Adjust salt. Dip the octopus in the boiling water, cover for 4 minutes with the lid, then remove it and leave it out for 2 minutes, then put it back into the pot and continue cooking for half an hour. Separately cook the peeled steamed potatoes. When cooked, remove the potatoes and the octopus, let them cool and cut into small pieces. Put everything in a bowl, season with oil, salt, pepper and chopped parsley.

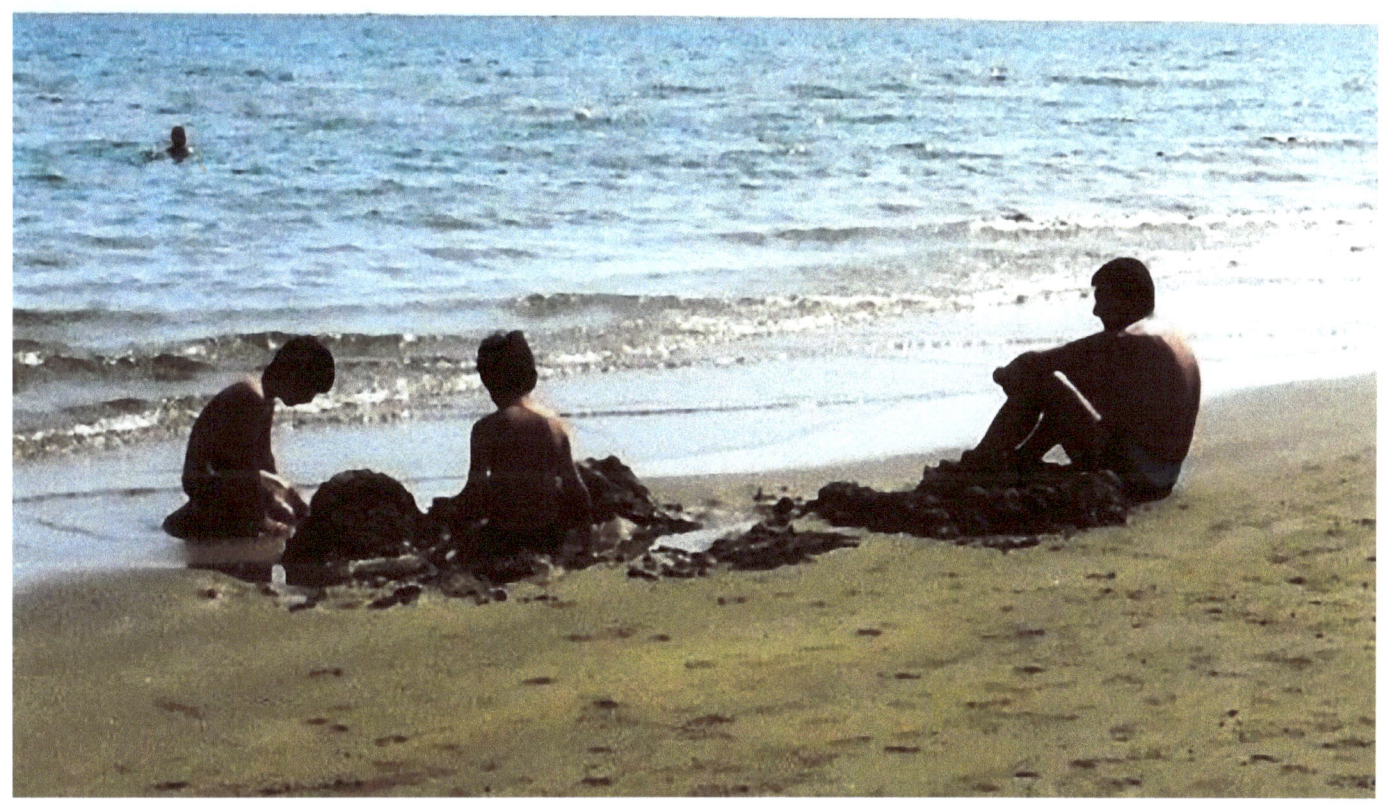

June

Orate al forno, *baked oratas*. Clean the sea breams well removing the scales. In a saucepan heat the oil with the thin slices of a lemon zest, rosemary, sage and bay leaf. When the oil is hot, add the oratas and brown them on both sides. Add the garlic and bake for ten minutes at 180 degrees. Remove them from oven, wet with vinegar and sprinkle with oregano. Remove the garlic and adjust with salt and pepper. Put them in the oven for another ten minutes, wetting them occasionally with their sauce. When cooked, remove the sea breams carefully and wet with a drizzle of raw oil. Accompany the dish with a fresh salad.

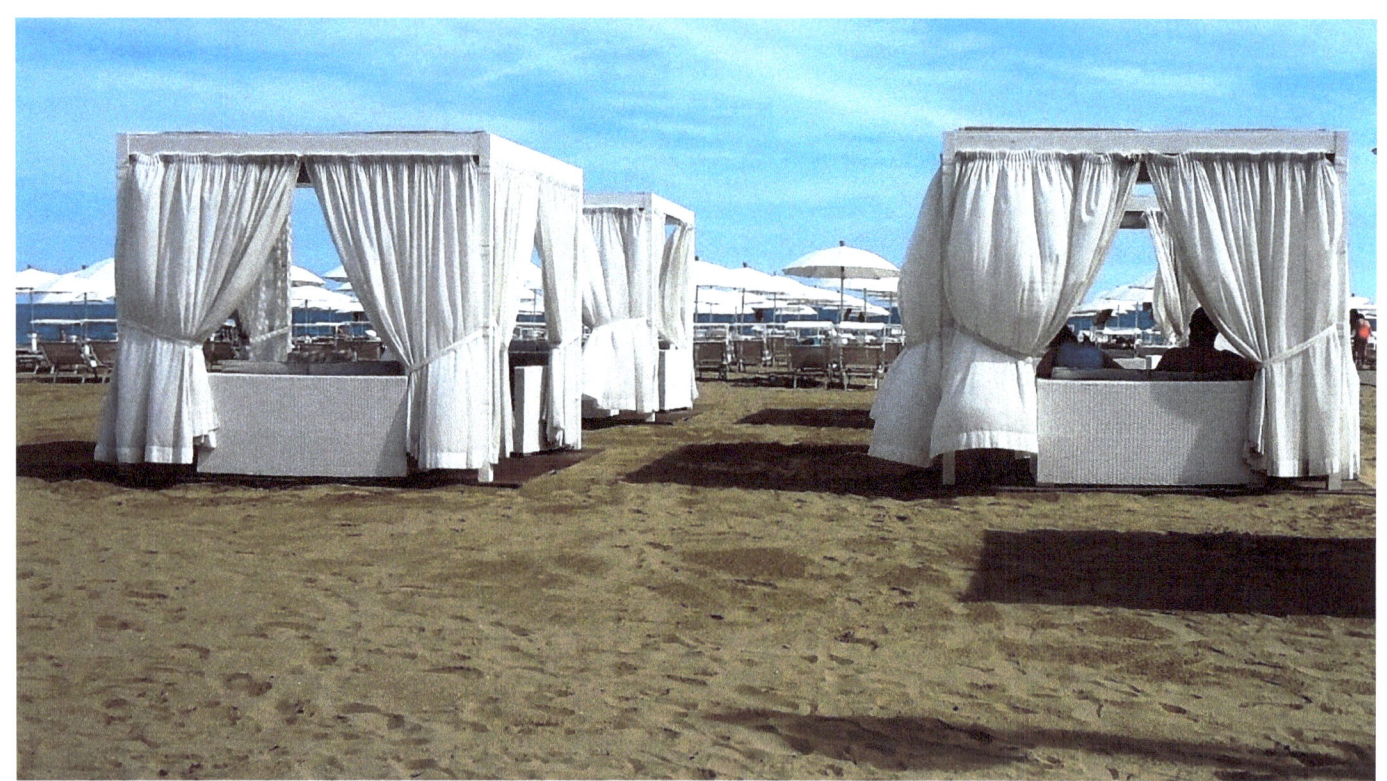
June

Pesce persico estivo, *summer perch*. Cut a courgette, a carrot and tomatoes into cubes. Cut the onion and fry in a pan with the oil, garlic and sage. Remove the garlic and put the fillets of perch to browning one minute on each side. Lower the heat, add the vegetables, season with salt and pepper and cook for ten minutes, turning the fillets halfway through cooking.

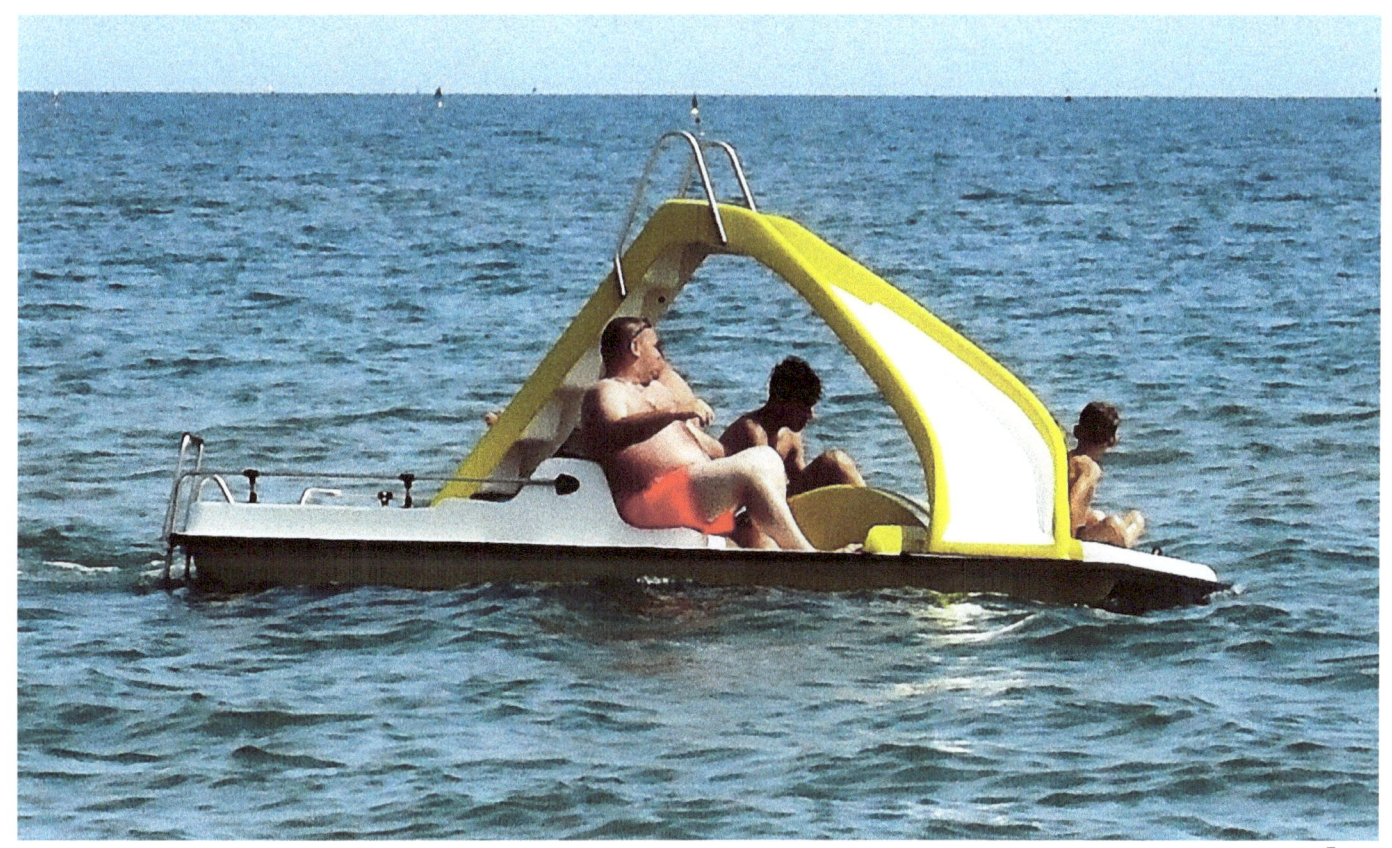

June

Salmone al salto, *salmon to the jump*. Lightly fry with an onion cut into slices, four cloves of garlic (to be removed later), oil, pepper and salt. Put in a pan about twenty olives and let them heat up for a while. Add the slices of salmon, making them sear quickly on both sides. Add the white wine and let it evaporate. Turn the salmon one time and it will be ready. One minute before removing it from the heat, sprinkle the slices of salmon with the juice of half an orange.

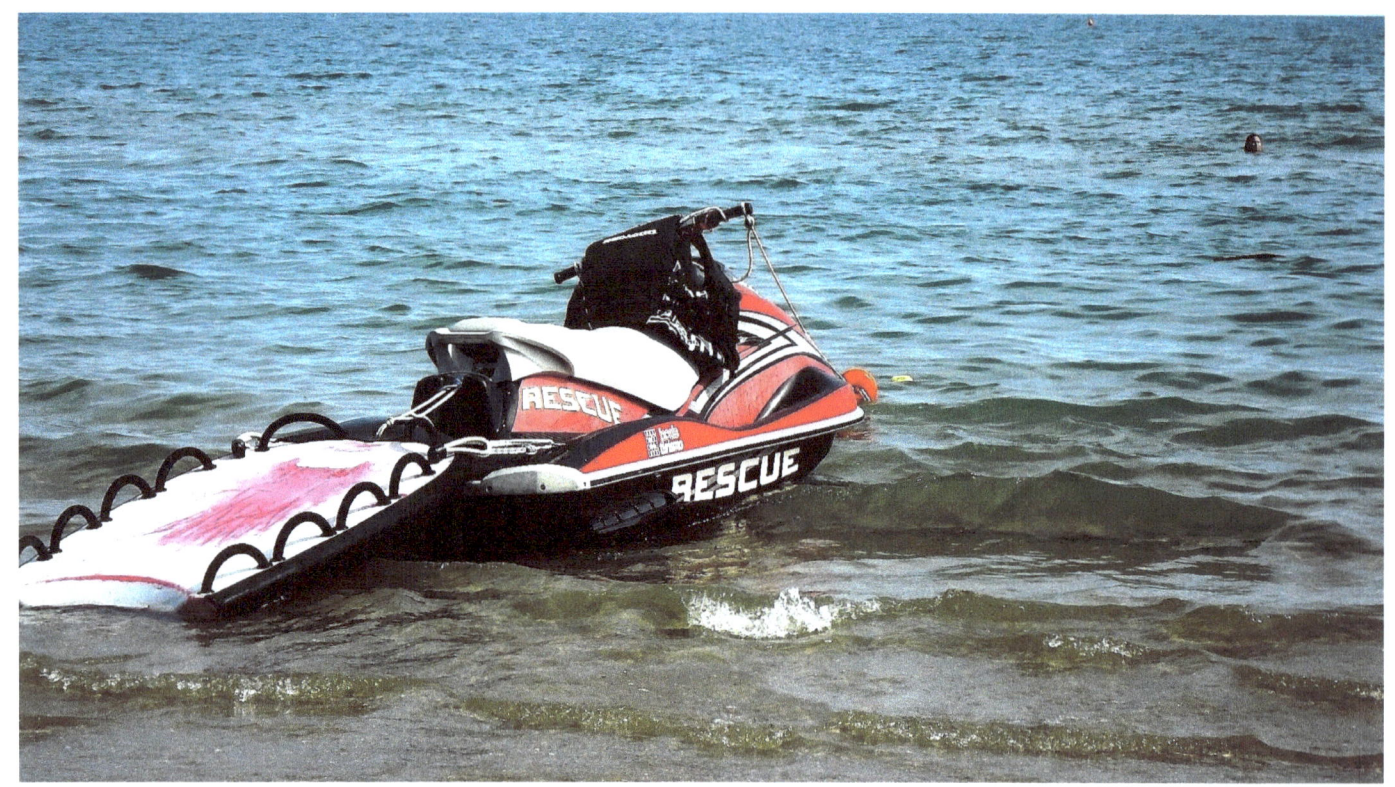

June

Salmone in crosta, *salmon in crust*. Wash and clean the salmon well. Knead the flour with water, but without salt. Make a dough of less than one centimeter of thickness a little longer than the fish and wide one and a half times, keeping aside a handful of pasta. Put on the same size of fish of the pastry several slices of onion and garlic, capers, parsley and slices of lemon. Put the salmon, fill the belly with the same aromas and salt. Repeat the same operation above the fish. Cover it with the pastry of the edges by shaping it on the shapes of salmon. With the advanced pasta form the other forms of fish such as the eye, scales etc. Finally brush it with the beaten egg.

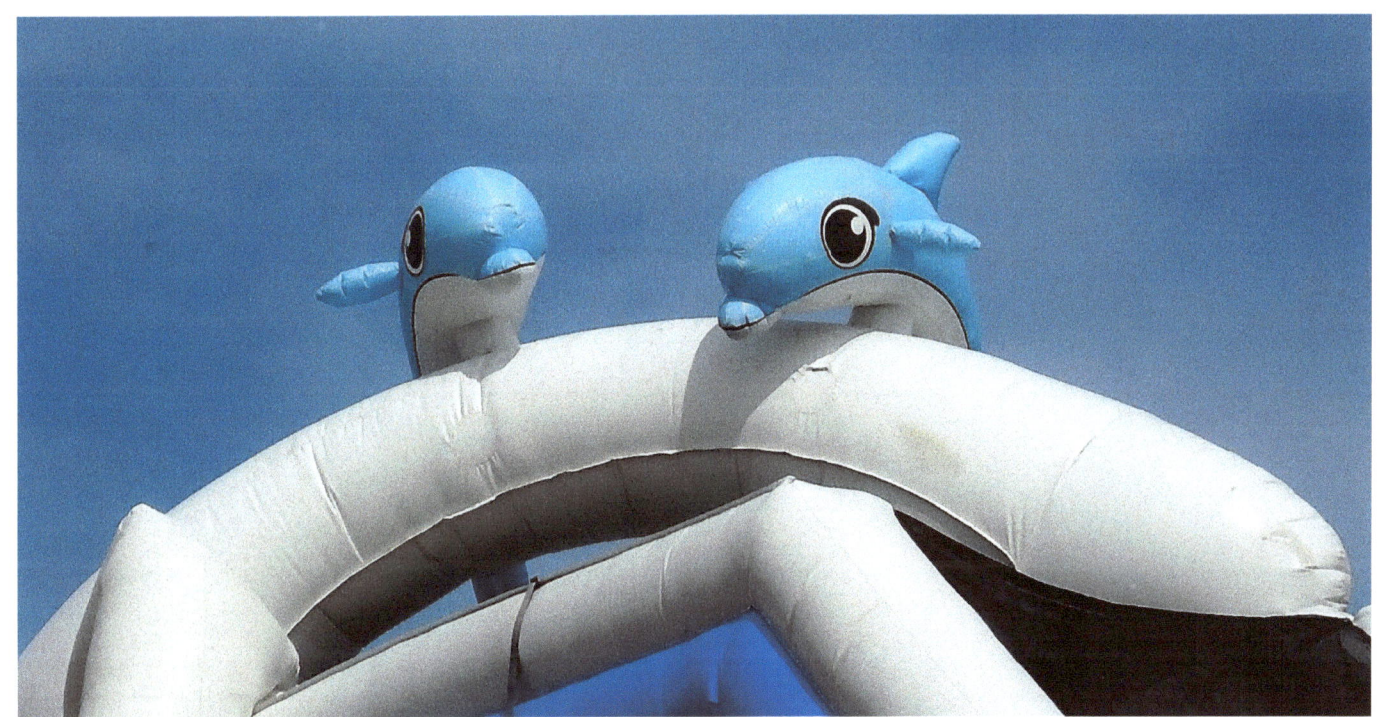
June

Sepie col pien, *stuffed cuttlefish*. Clean the cuttlefish thoroughly by removing the bone, the head and the bag with the ink. Wash them carefully. Chop the head and the tentacles and mix the mixture obtained in a bowl together with the breadcrumbs, previously soaked in milk and squeezed, garlic, parsley, parmesan cheese, beaten egg, salt and pepper. Fill the cuttlefish with the dough and close the bag entrance with string. Fry them in oil for a few minutes, sprinkling them with the white wine. Finally add the chopped tomatoes and a little salt. Bake in a baking dish for half an hour and serve with hot polenta.

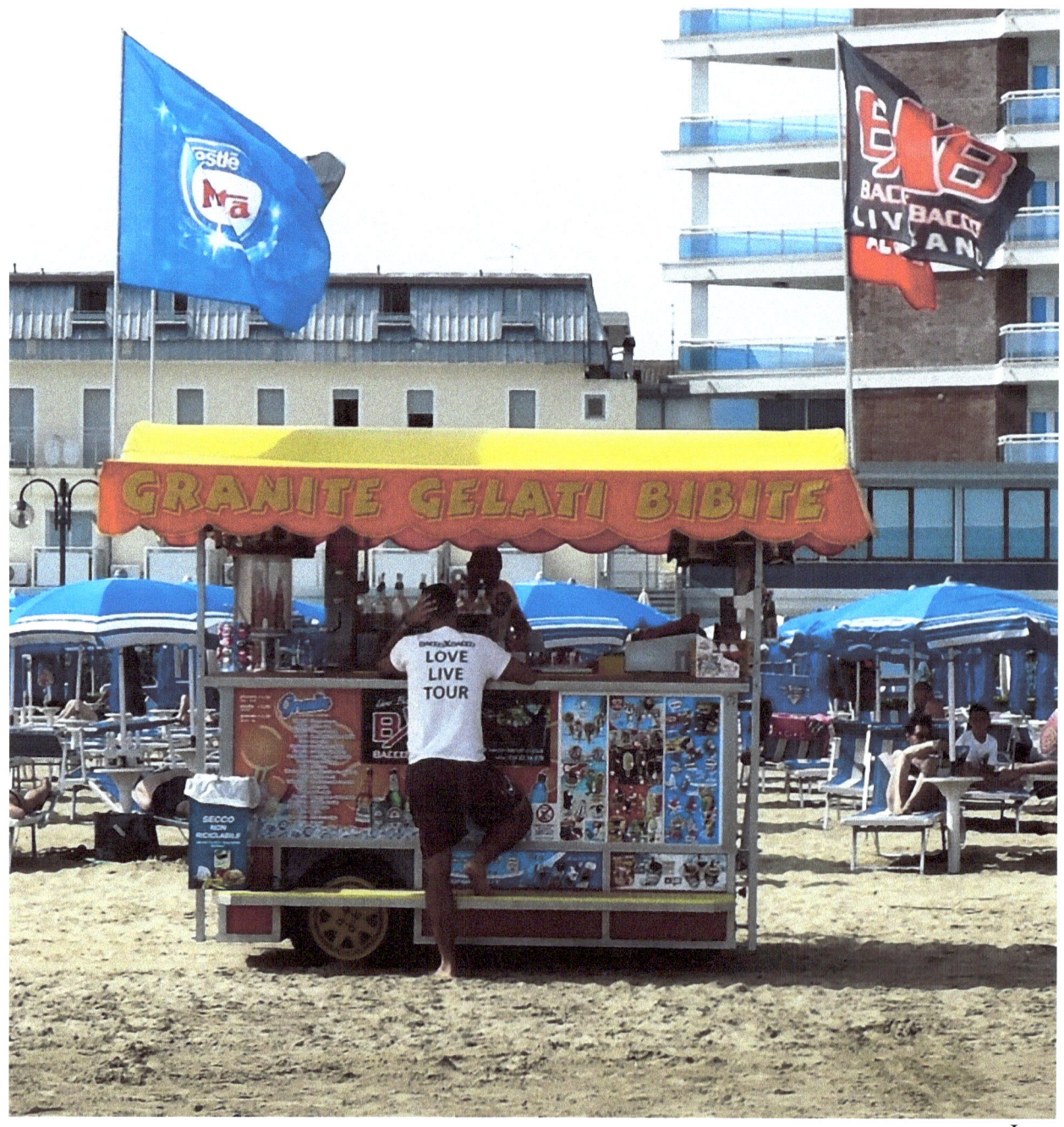

June

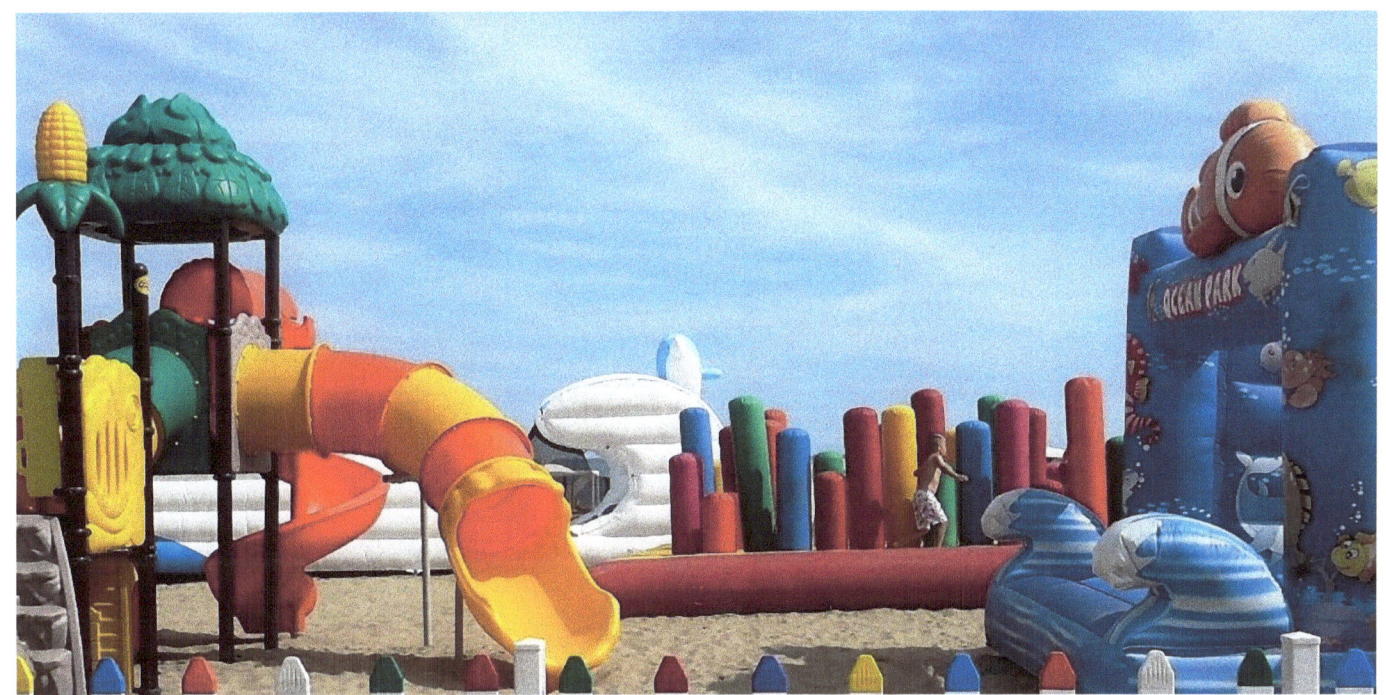

June

Sepie in umido, *cuttlefish stewed*. Prepare a sauté with a finely chopped onion and two cloves of garlic (to be removed later). Clean the cuttlefish and cut into small pieces. Pour them in the pan turning them over for a few minutes. Sprinkle with white wine and let it evaporate, then pour abundant peeled tomatoes. Finish cooking, adjust salt and serve hot with white polenta.

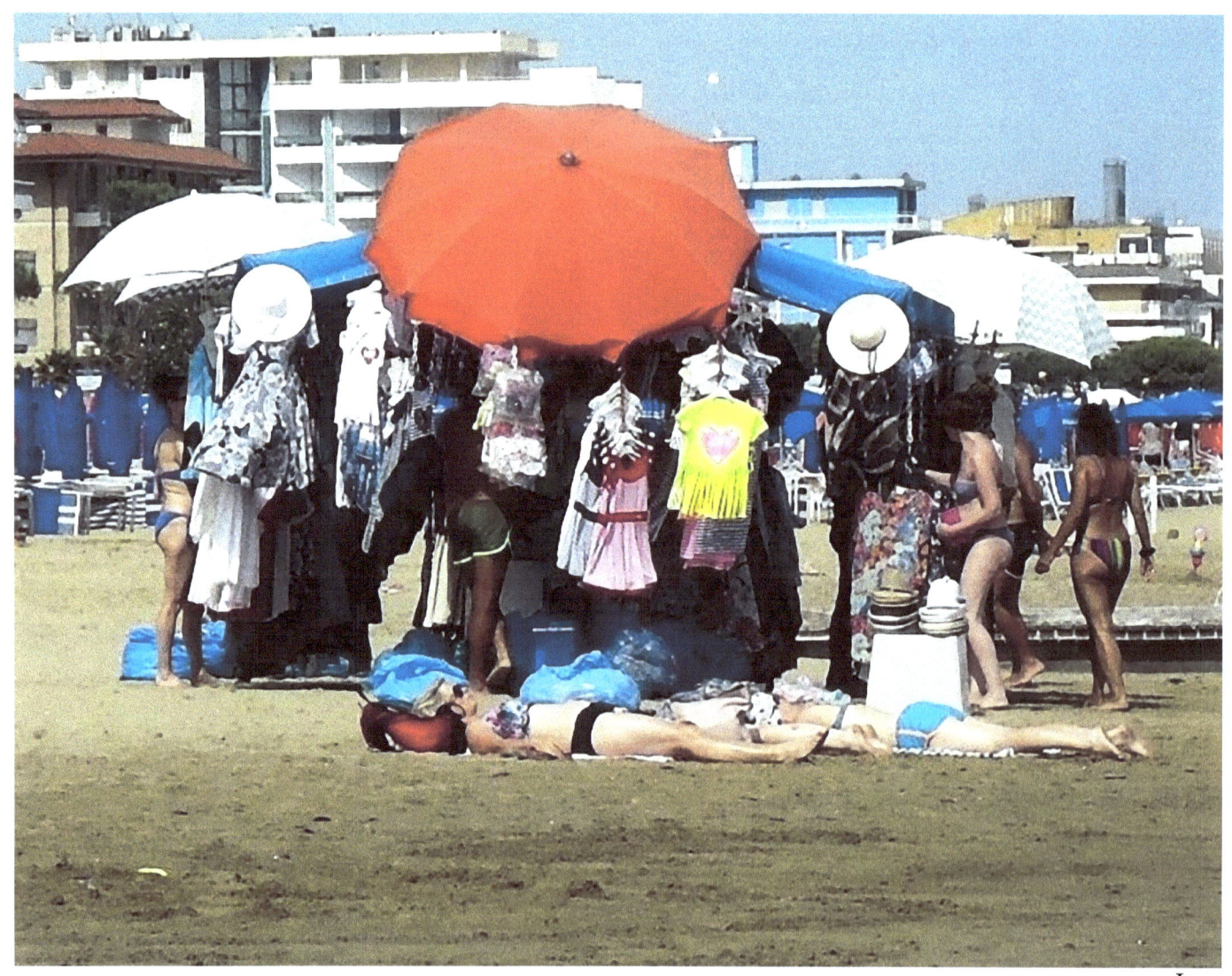

June

Salsina nera, *black sauce*. Mix together the mayonnaise, the black olive paste and a pinch of powdered red pepper.

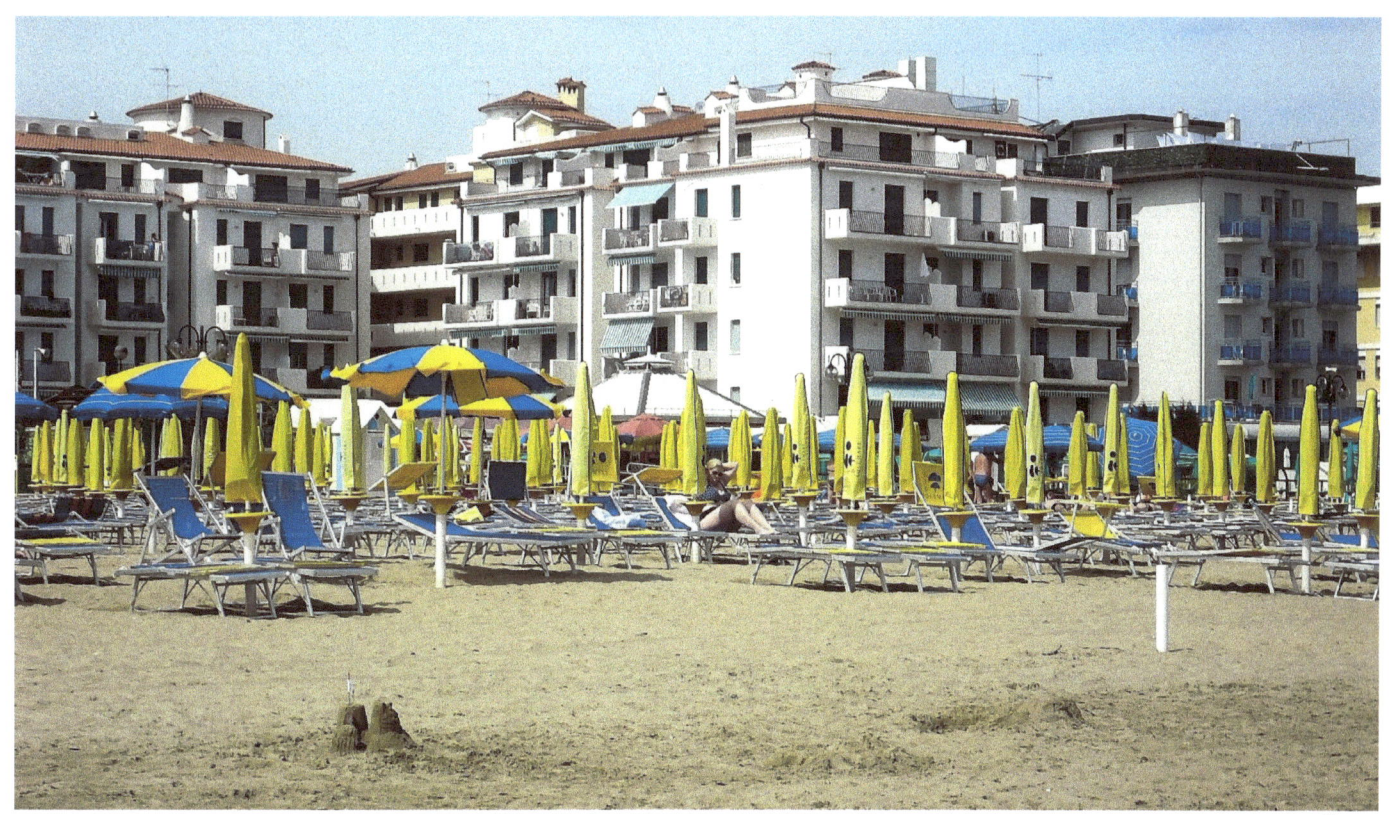

June

Salsa verde, *green sauce*. Mix together the mayonnaise, the horseradish, the capers, the minced garlic and parsley and grated cheese.

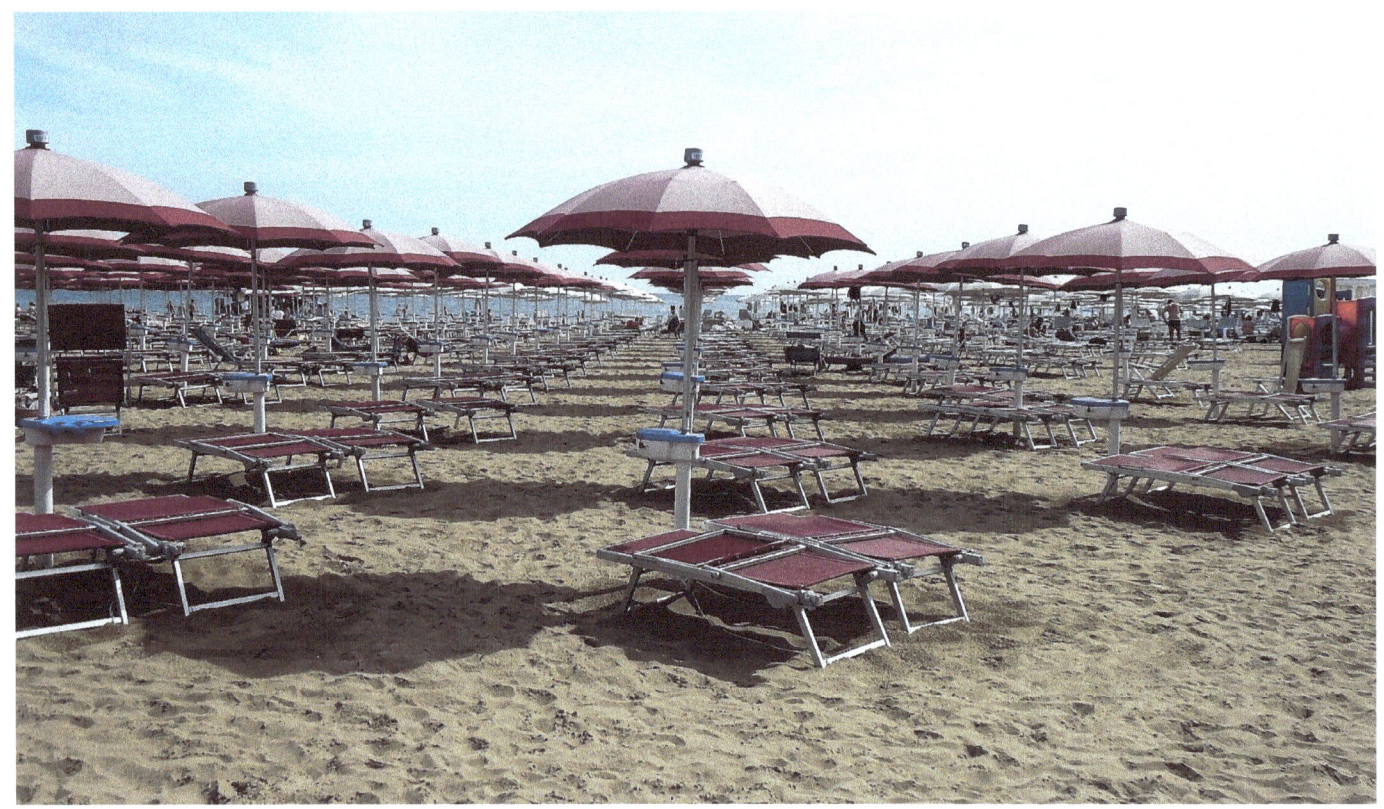

June

Baìcoli, *crunchy biscuits*. Dissolve the brewer's yeast in half a glass of warm milk and knead it with 100g of flour. Let rise for half an hour and in the meantime whisk the egg white of an egg. Mix 300g of flour with sugar and a pinch of salt, add the leavened dough from before, the egg whites and 70g of butter at room temperature. Knead for about ten minutes adding if you need lukewarm milk. Divide the dough into 4 parts and cut into strips of 8 cm in diameter. Arrange them in a cooking plate and let them rise for a couple of hours covered with a cloth. Bake at 180 degrees for 15 minutes until golden brown. Remove them from the oven as they are and cover them with the tea towel. Let them rest for a couple of days, then slice them sideways as if they were salami, making them take their characteristic shape and bake them again for about 10 minutes, observing them continuously.

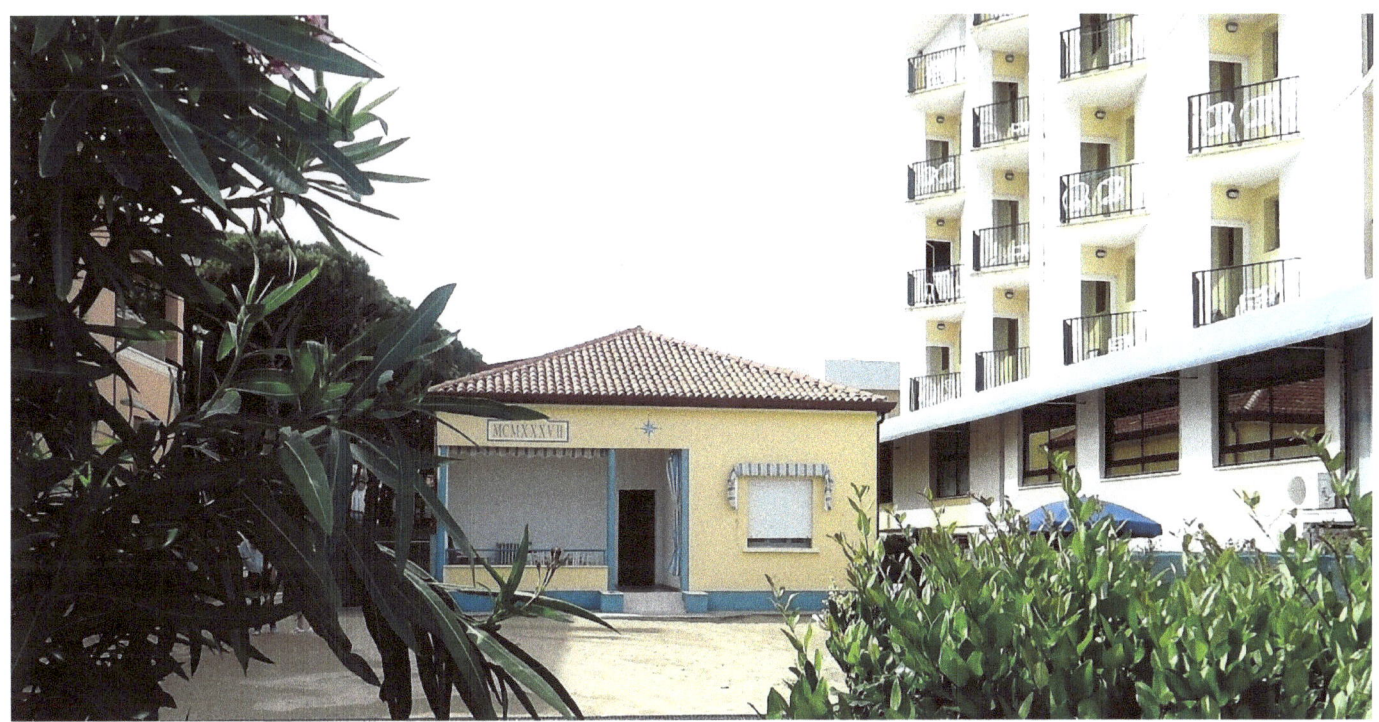
June

Bigarani. Melt 100g of butter in a bain-marie and crumble 50g of brewer's yeast in a glass of warm milk. Beat 3 egg yolks with a pinch of salt, keeping the egg white aside. Place 500g of flour in the fountain and pour the beaten eggs into the hollow, the milk with the yeast, 100g of sugar and melted butter. Work the dough for a long time with your hands, then cover it with a cloth and let it rise in a warm place. After 3 hours, knead the dough again in order to obtain loaves with a length of about 20 cm and about 1.5 cm of diameter. Roll them almost in half by twisting a bit inwards and place them spaced on a baking tray. Bake at 150 degrees C for 15 minutes, then remove the plate from the oven, brush biscuits with the egg white and leave to rest overnight. In the morning, put the biscuits in the oven for 15-20 minutes to toast them.

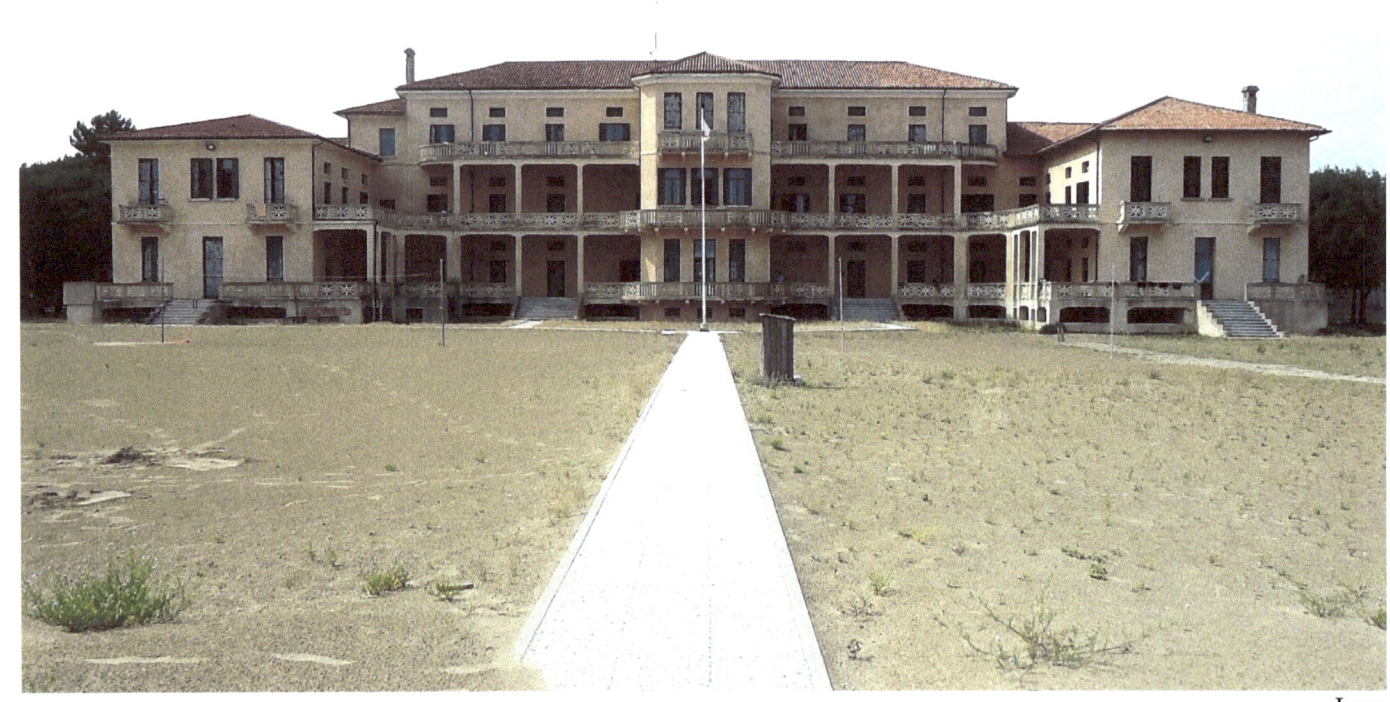

June

Essi buranèi, *s-shaped biscuits from Burano*. In a bowl combine 150g of butter at room temperature with 300g of sugar, then add one at a time six eggs mixing well, two sachets of vanillin, the juice of a lemon, a drop of rum and salt. Finally pour a little at a time 500g of white flour and continue the final dough with your hands. Made of thin strips, about ten centimeters long and about the size of a finger, to form the characteristic (or in the form of a donut). Bake at 180 degrees for about 20 minutes. The "essi" can be consumed alone as common biscuits or as desserts accompanied with sweet and liqueur wine.

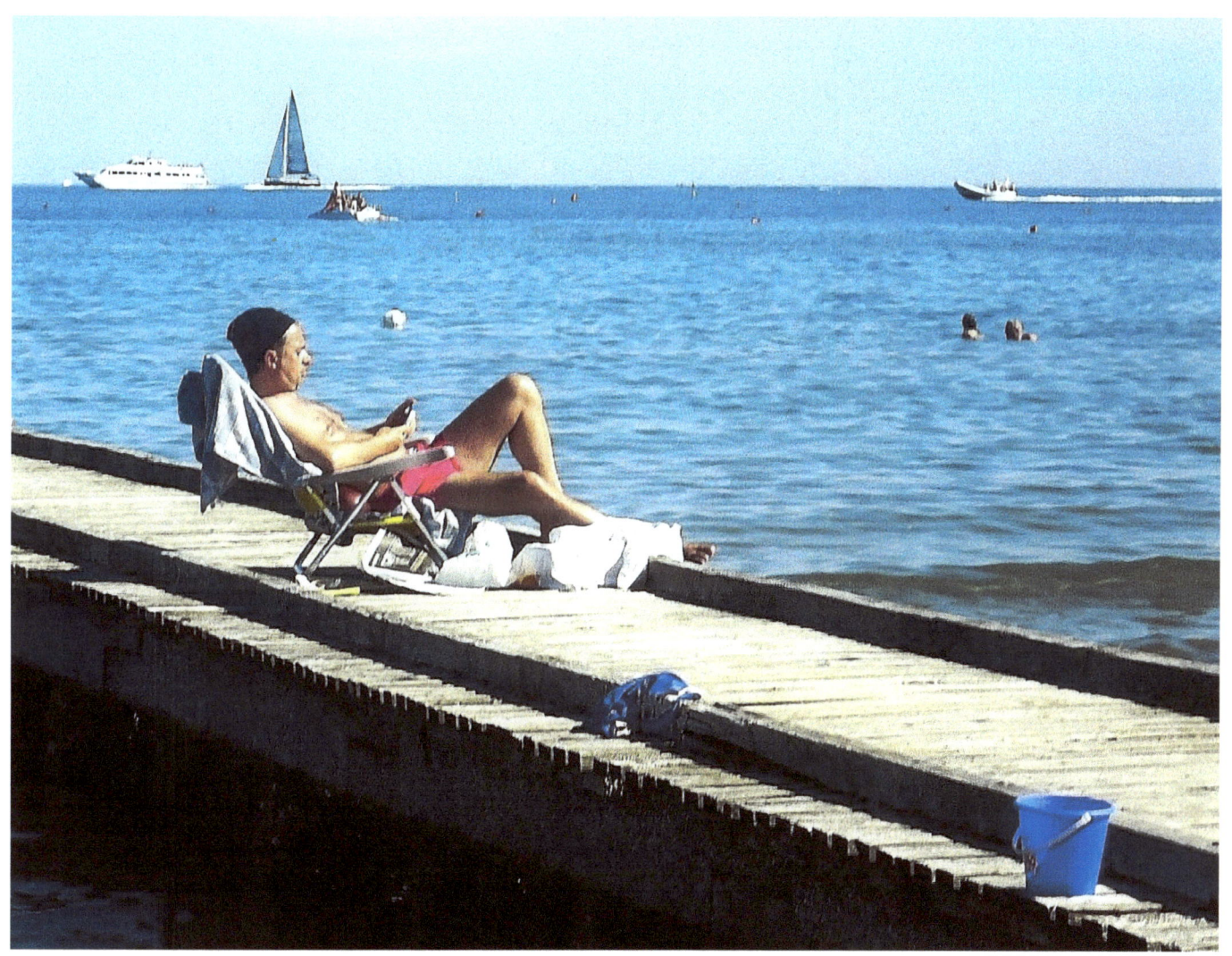

June

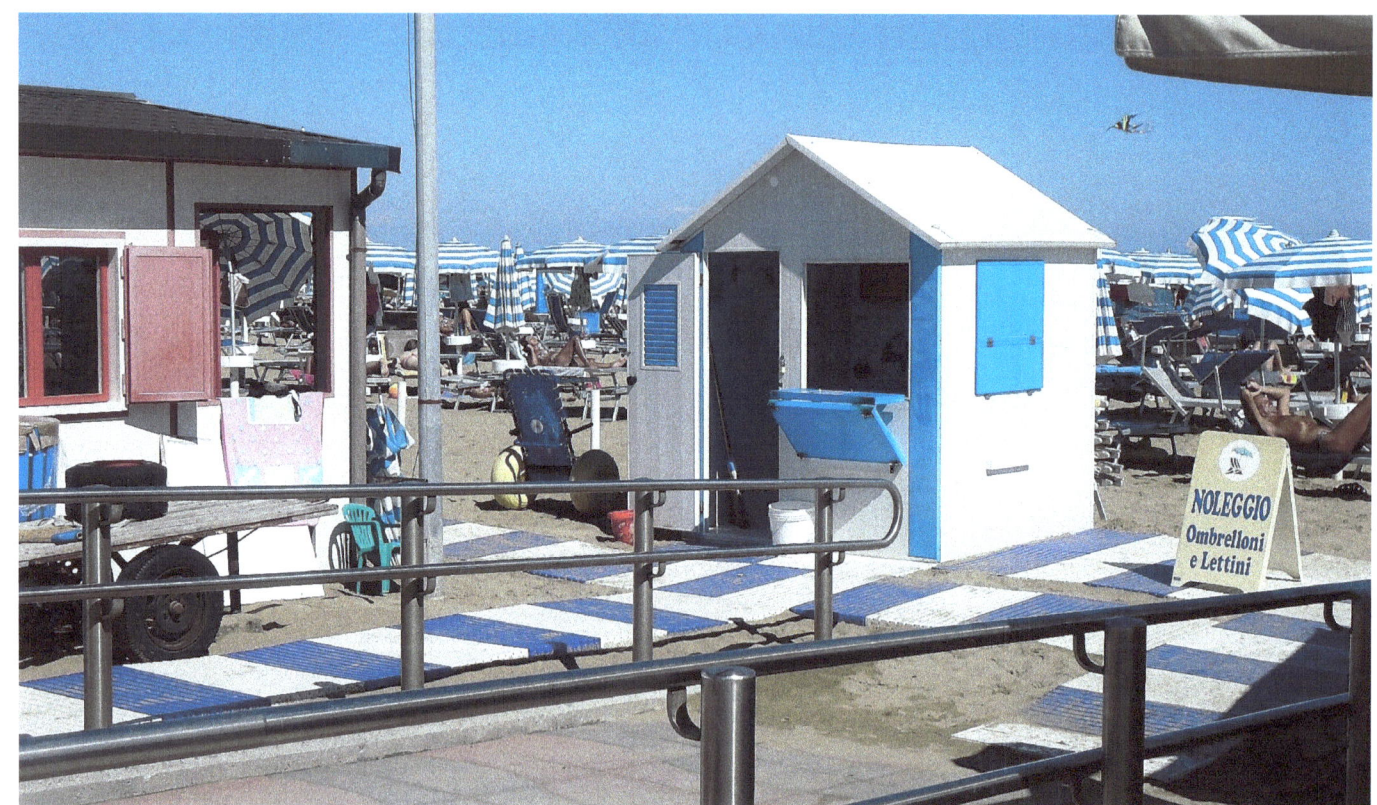

June

Fritoe aea venessiana, *Venetian pancakes*. In a cup, put 130g of raisins in the grappa. Dilute 40g of brewer's yeast in half a glass of warm water. In a bowl mix 500g of flour, 2 eggs, milk, 80g of granulated sugar, the rind of a lemon, a pinch of cinnamon and one of salt. Mix well and add the melted brewer's yeast and the raisins with the grappa. Cover with a cloth and let stand for a few hours in a warm place. After rising, stir again and add milk if you want to obtain a more fluid mixture. In a pan heat the seed oil (or lard) and pour the batter into spoonfuls. At the end, once put on the serving dish, sprinkle with the vanilla sugar.

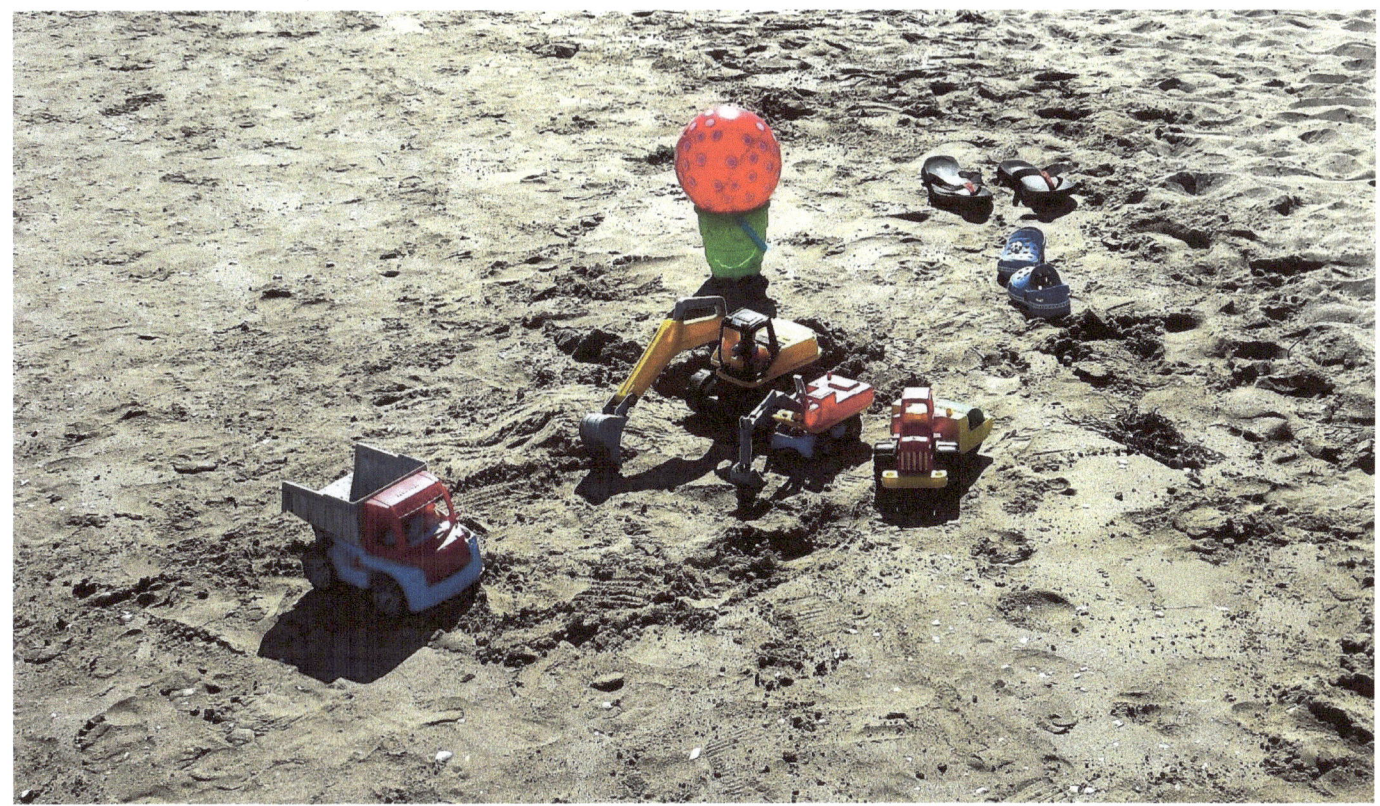
June

Pinsa. Cut the bread into small pieces, put it in a bowl, pour 6dl of milk and let it soak for at least half an hour. Soften 100g raisins in lukewarm water and beat two eggs. Slowly add 100g of flour, 100g of sugar, 30g of butter at room temperature, raisins, beaten eggs, a pinch of salt and mix everything. Grease and sprinkle a pan with a high edge, add the mixture and spread the fennel seeds on the surface. Bake at 180 degrees in an oven already hot for almost an hour. Leave it to cool in the mold, then remove from it and serve.

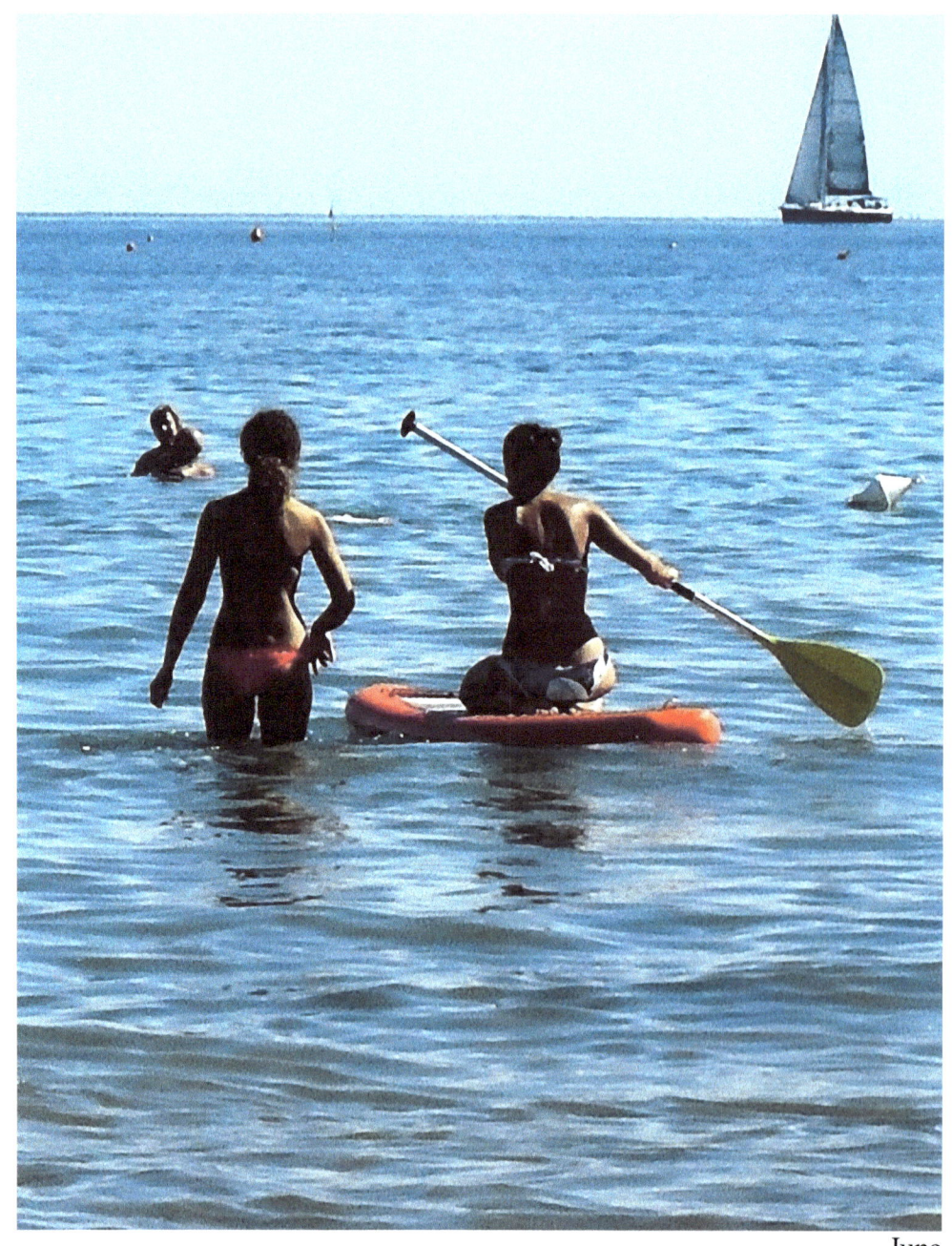

June

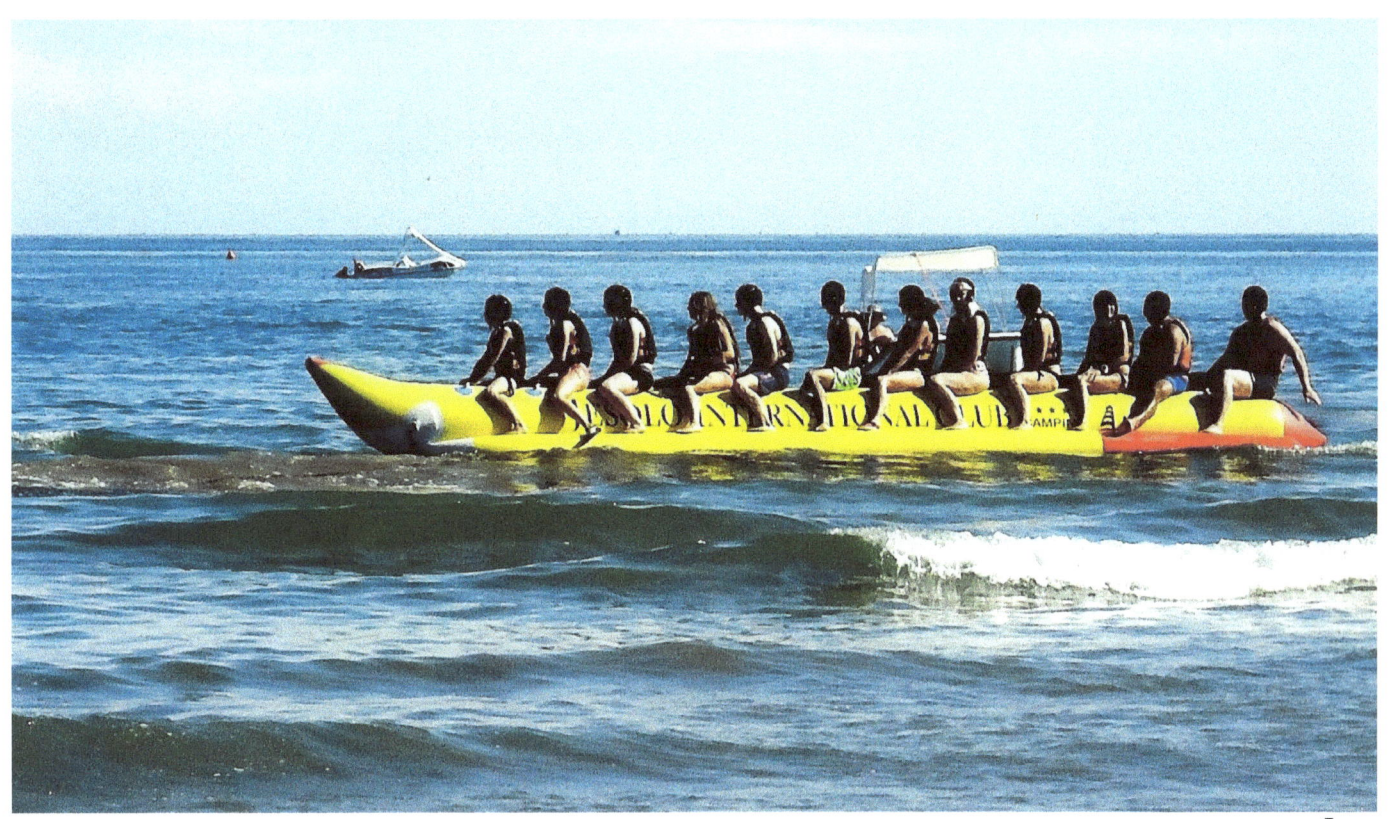

June

Zabaione, *zabaglione*. In a saucepan, beat with a wooden spoon 8 egg yolks and 12 tablespoons of sugar until you get a yellow foam, add 3dl of marsala, two pinches of cinnamon and mix well. Heat over very low heat stirring in the same direction until the mixture begins to rise but being careful not to let it boil otherwise will separate.

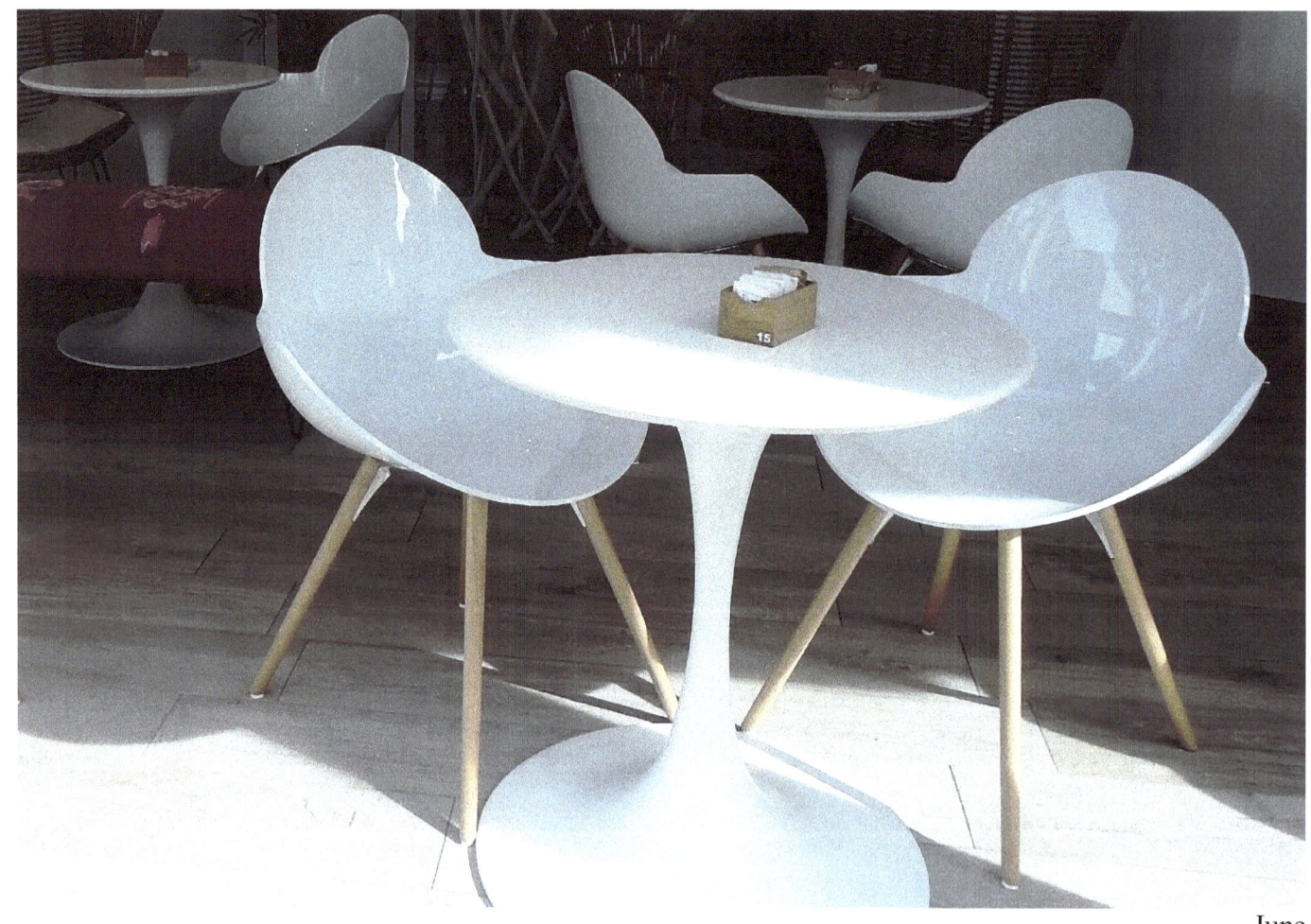

June

Zaeti. Mix together 350g of yellow flour and 250g of white flour with a pinch of yeast and add 100g of sugar to butter. Add 90g of raisins, preferably first softened in water, a glass of milk, 70g pine nuts, vanilla, lemon zest and stir until a soft dough. Form small ovals, about 10 cm long, arrange them on a previously buttered oven plate and bake them in a hot oven for about 25 minutes.

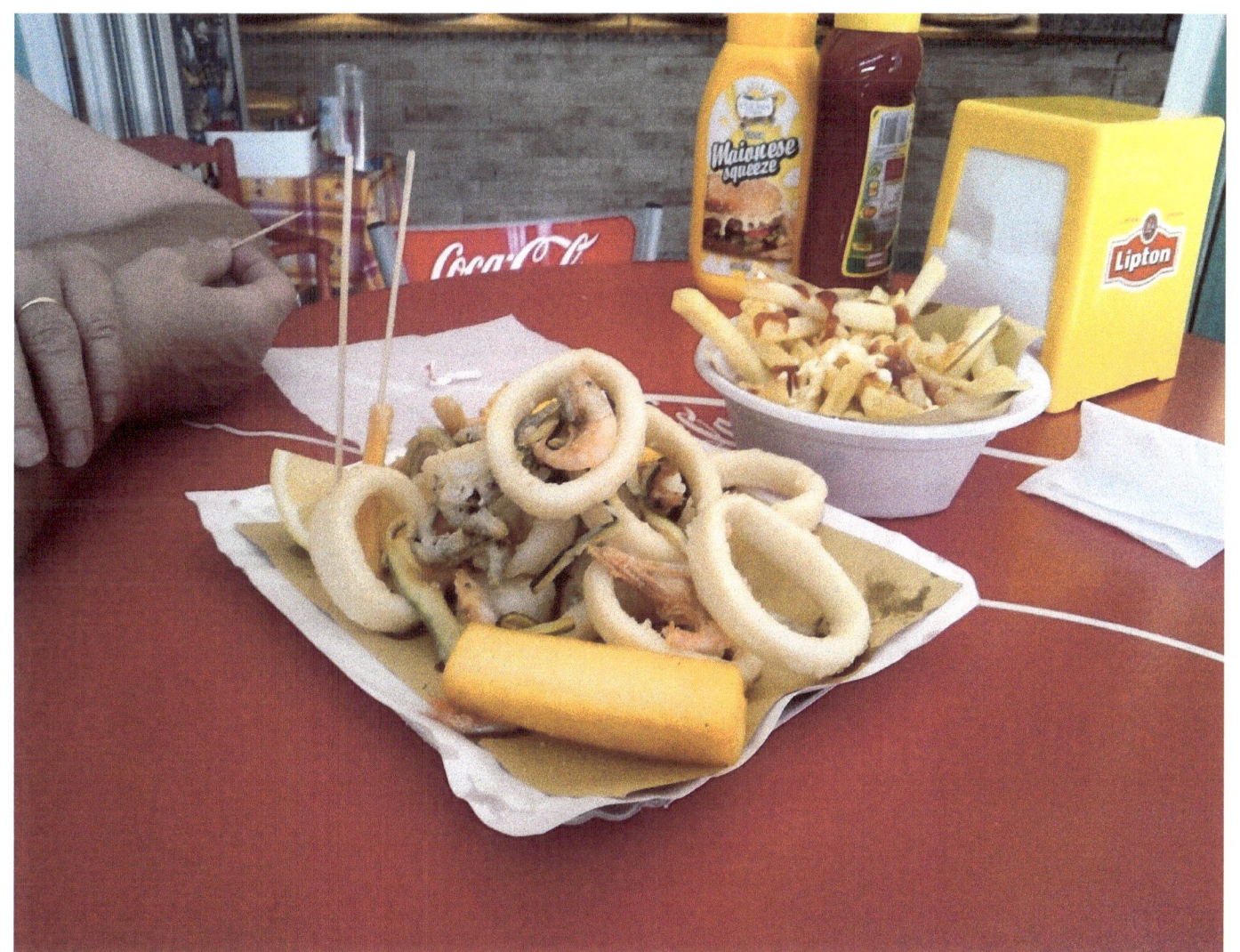

July

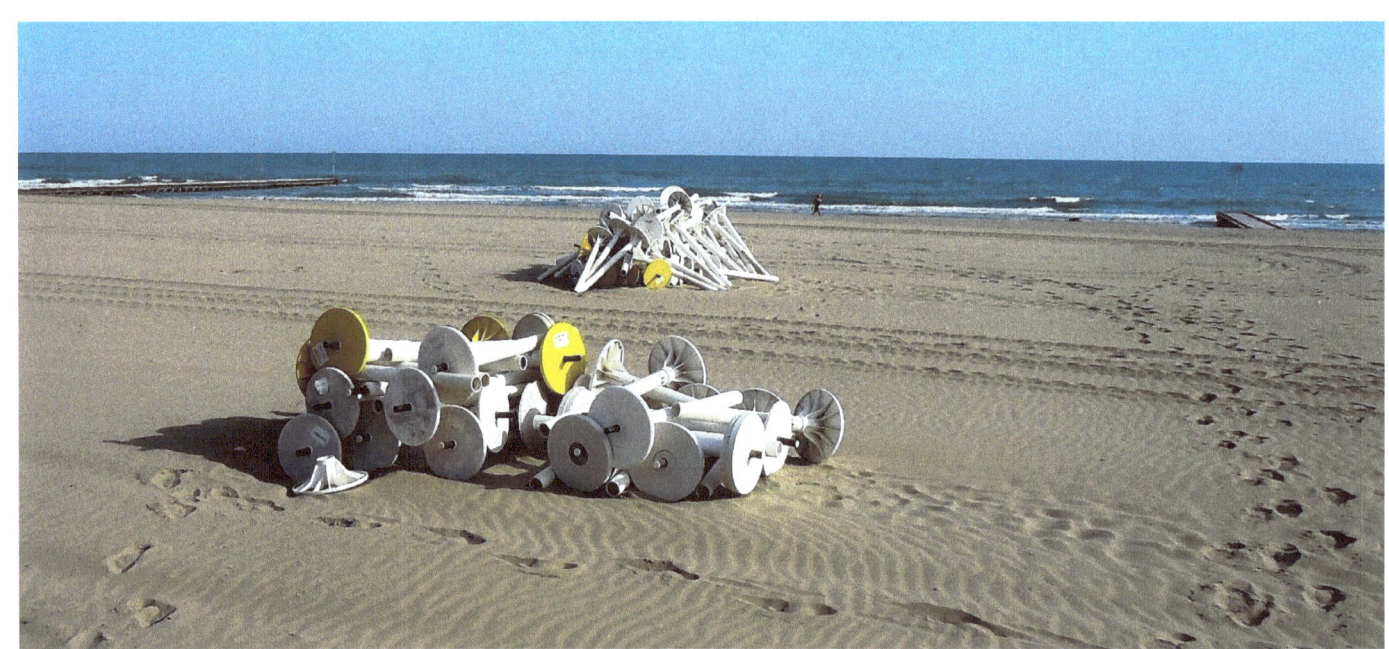

September

Rosolio. Crush 40g of fresh red rose petals in a mortar, add 100g of sugar, make a paste and put it to macerate for 10 days with 25dl of alcohol, pouring it into a glass jar. After this period of time, prepare a hot syrup using half a liter of water and 1500g of sugar, then let it cool and add it to the maceration jar. Stir, plug and leave to rest for another ten days. At the end of the established period, carefully filter, bottle, cap and store in a dark and cool place. Rosolio can be prepared with violet, lemon balm, cinnamon, cloves, lemon, mandarin.

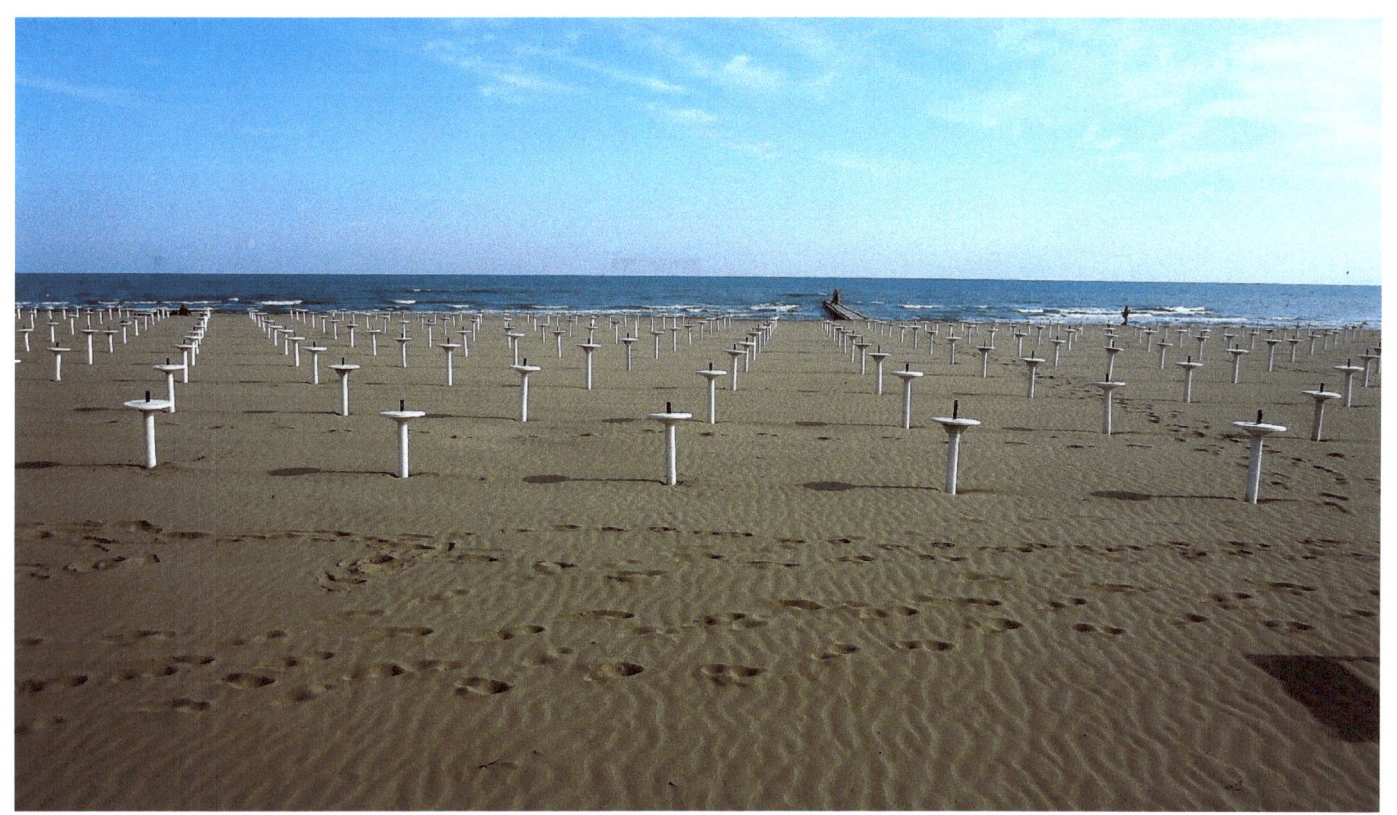

September

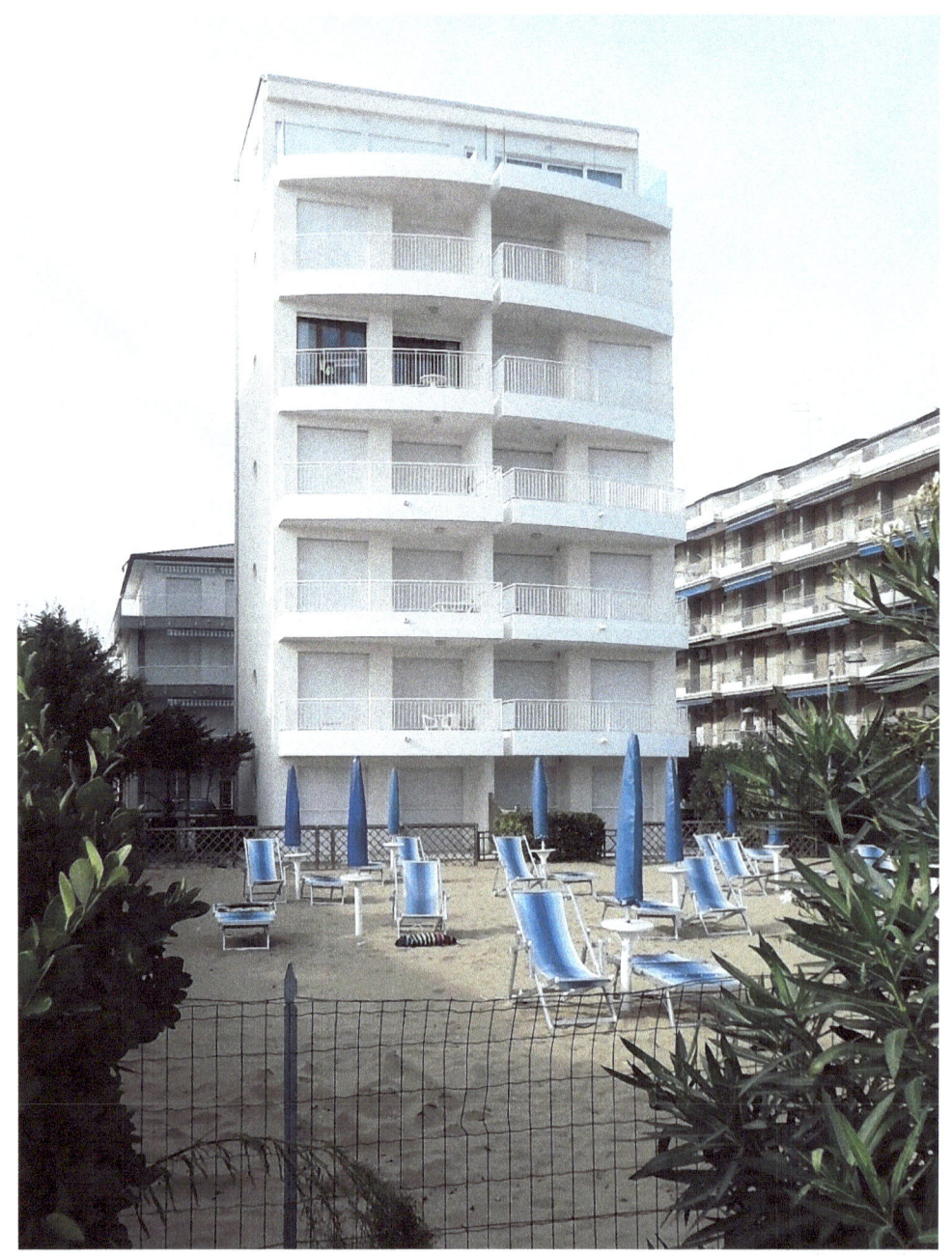

September

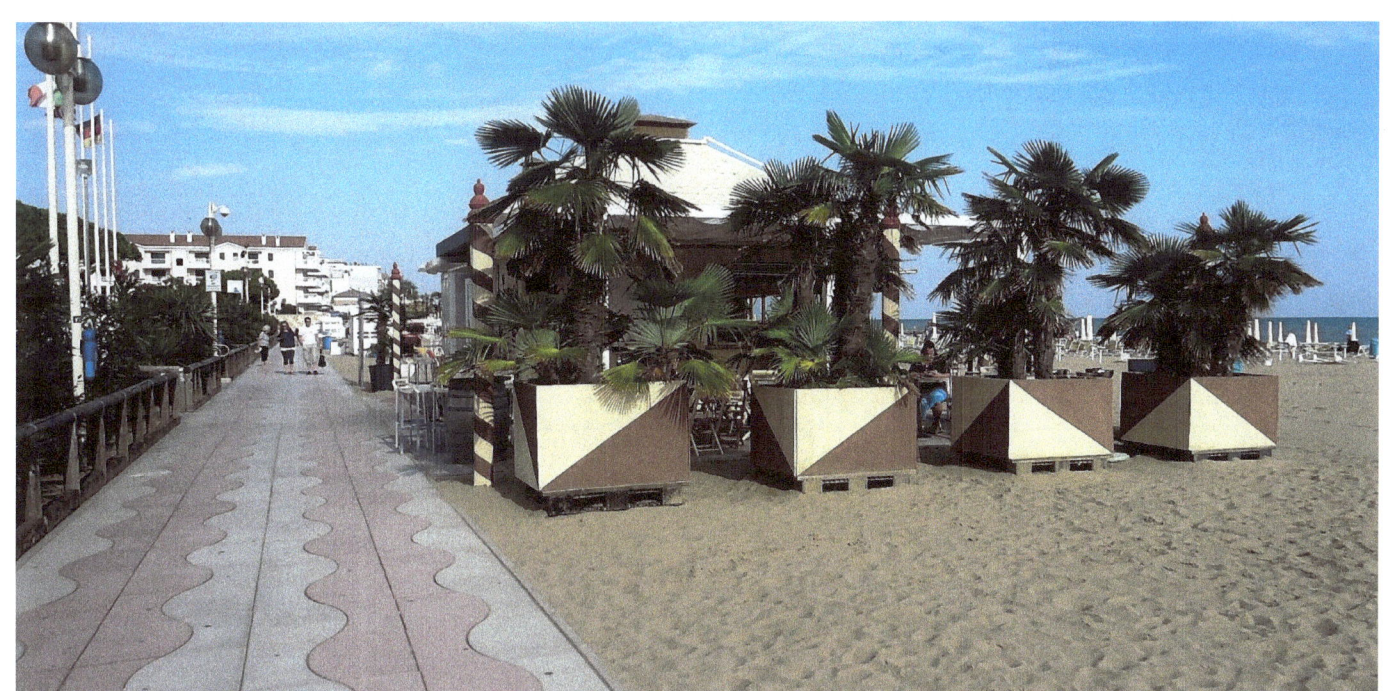

September

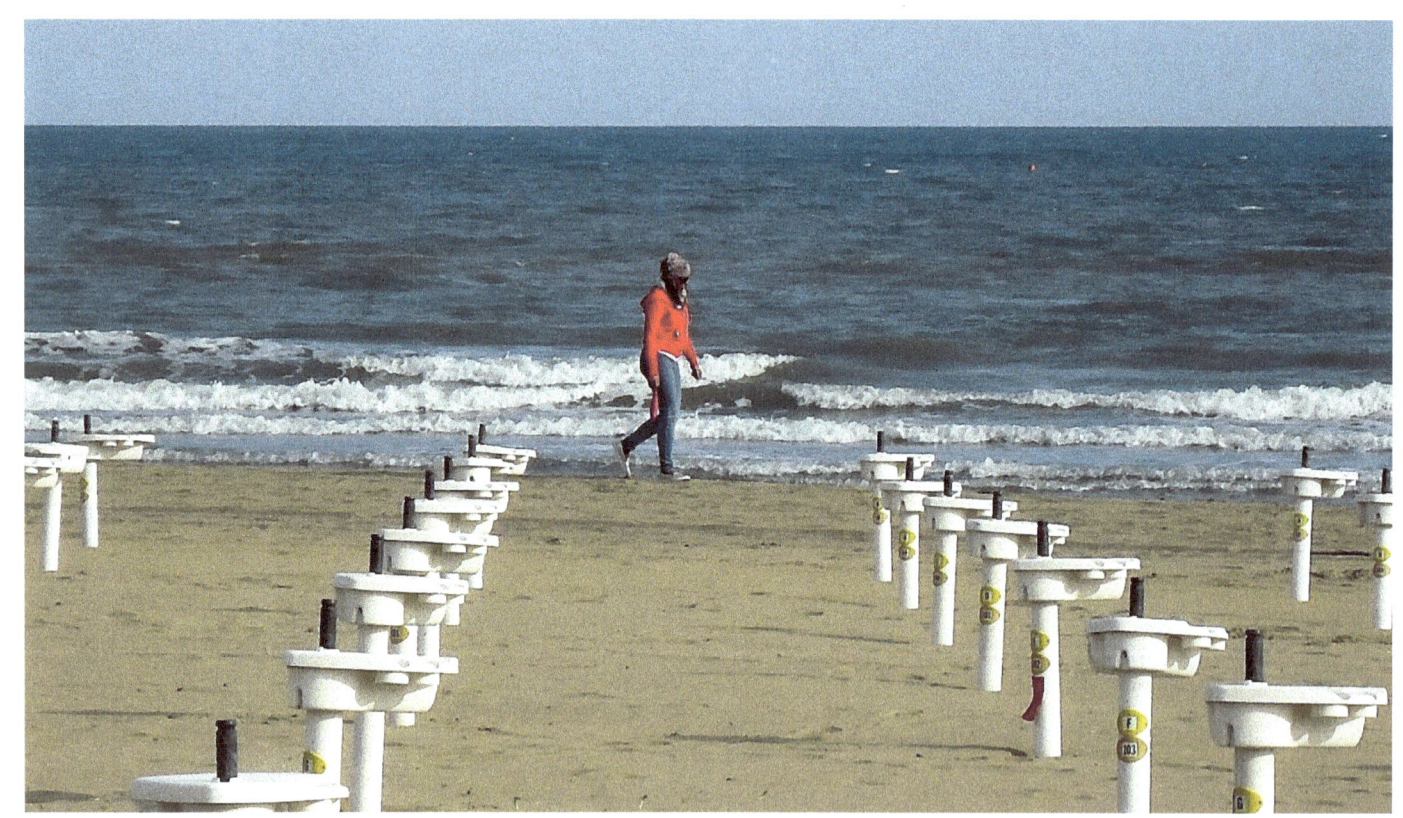

September

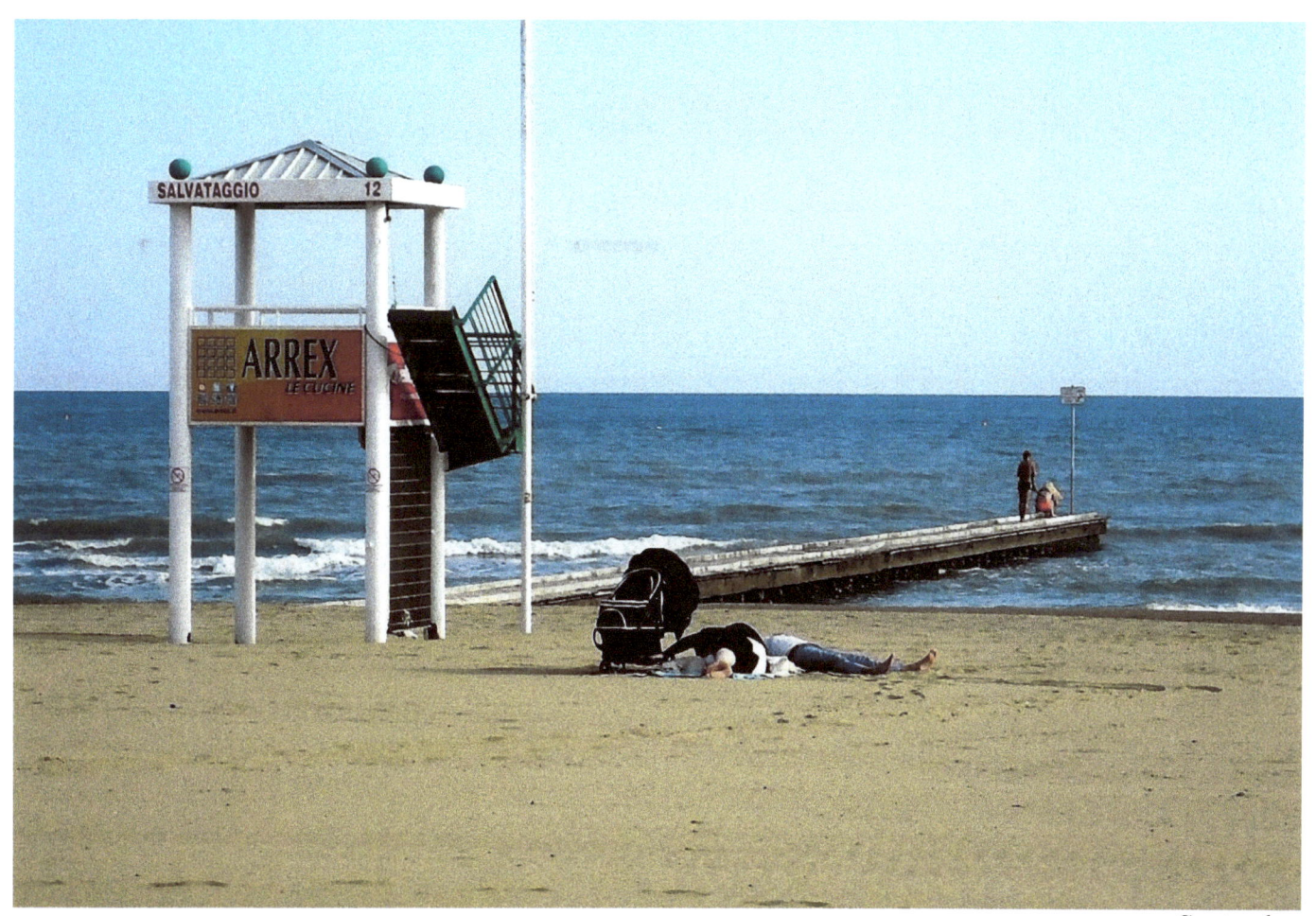

September

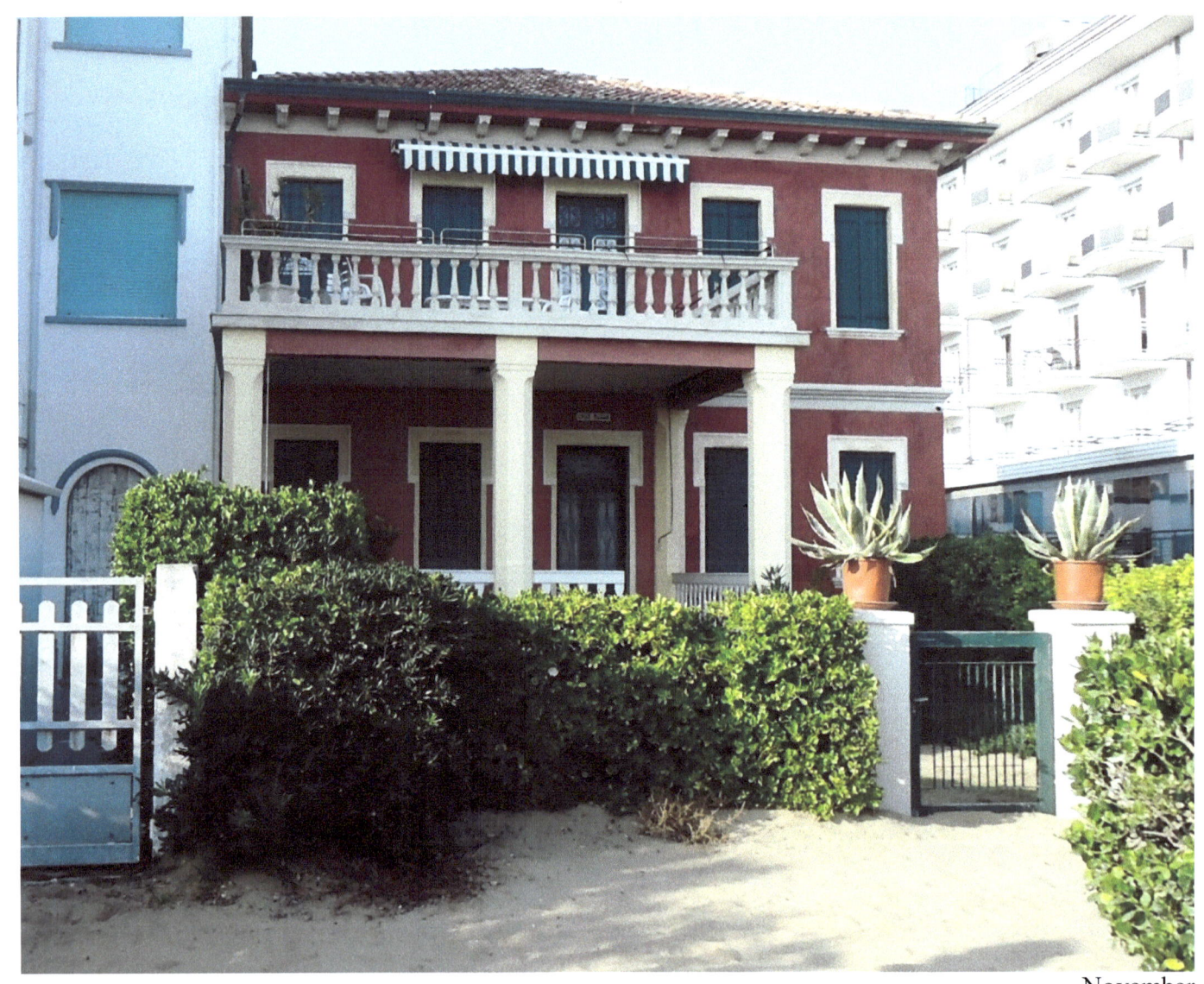

November

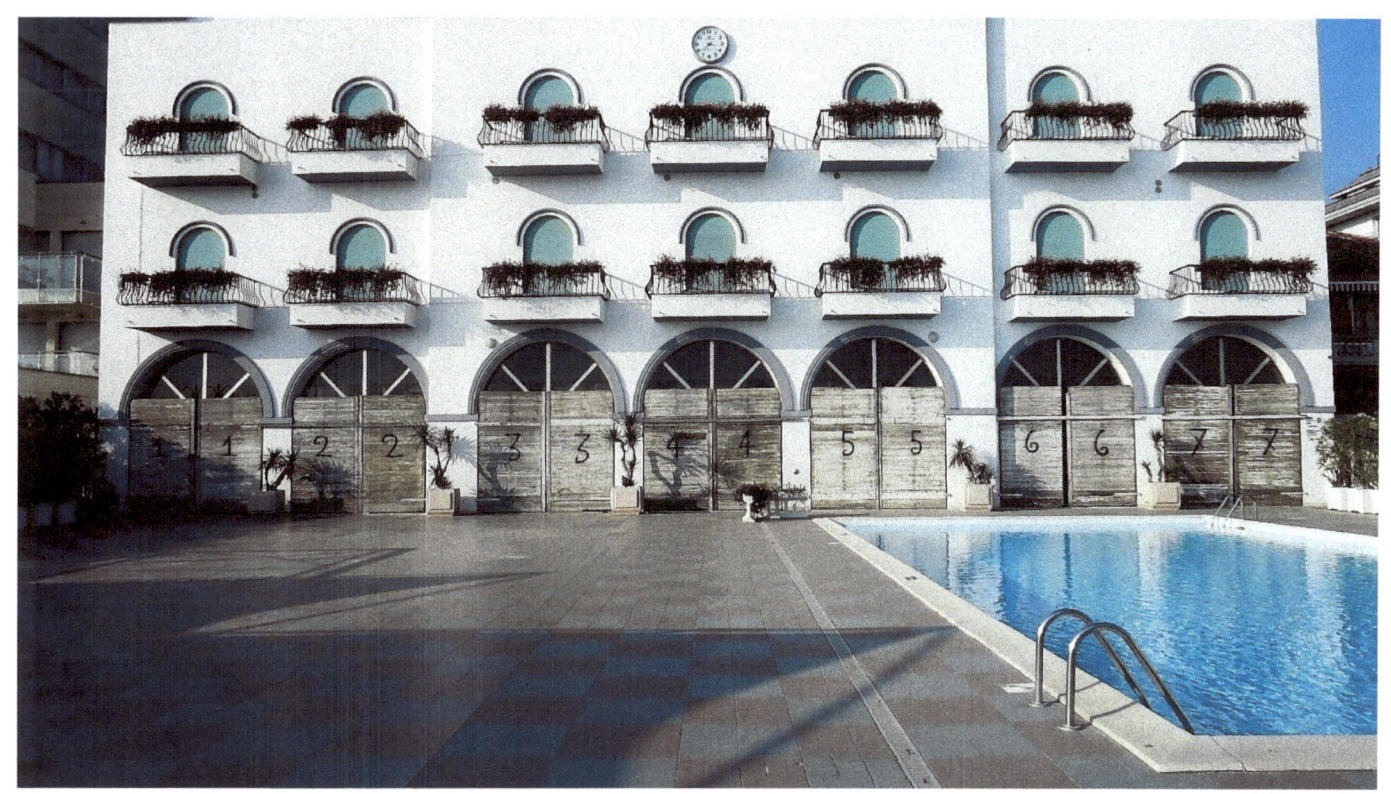
November

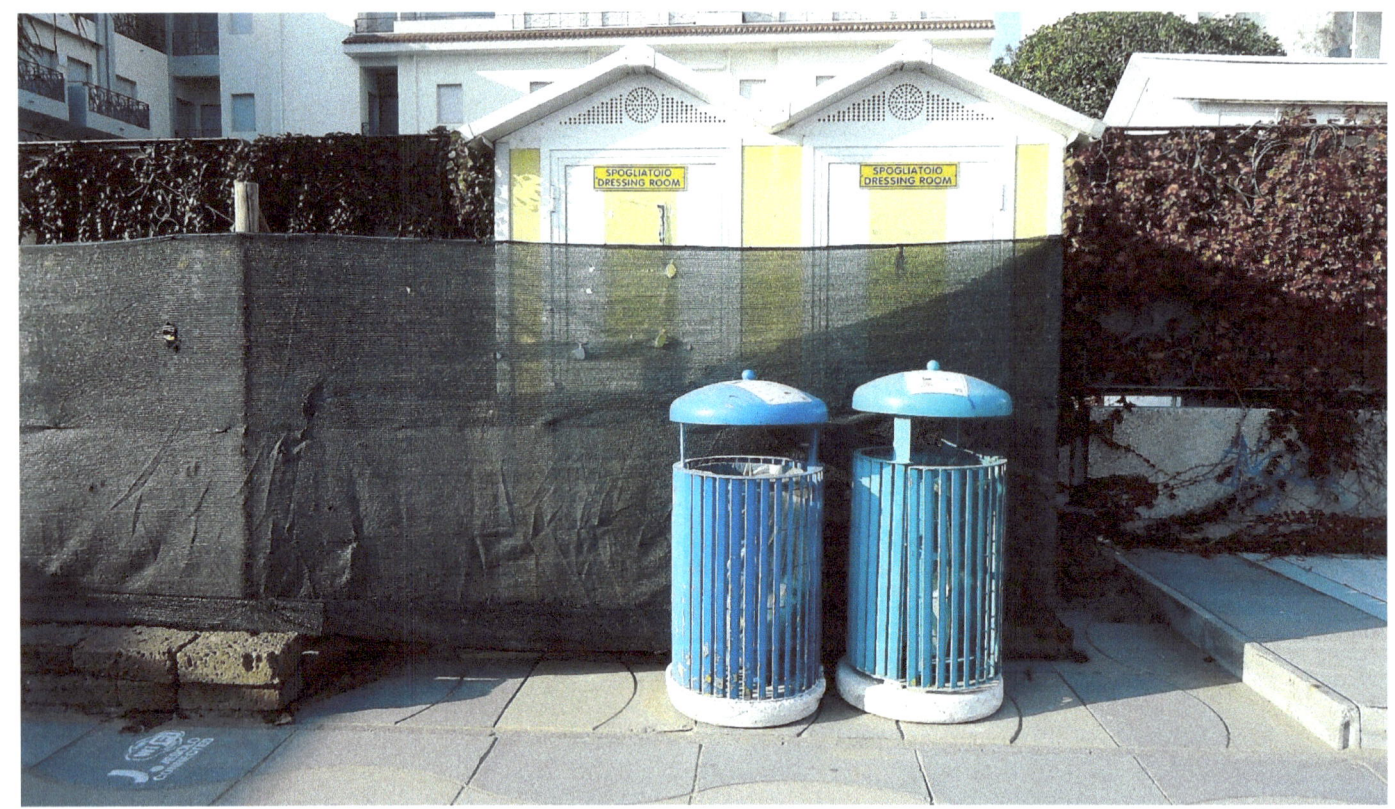

November

In the background the Torre Aquileia   November

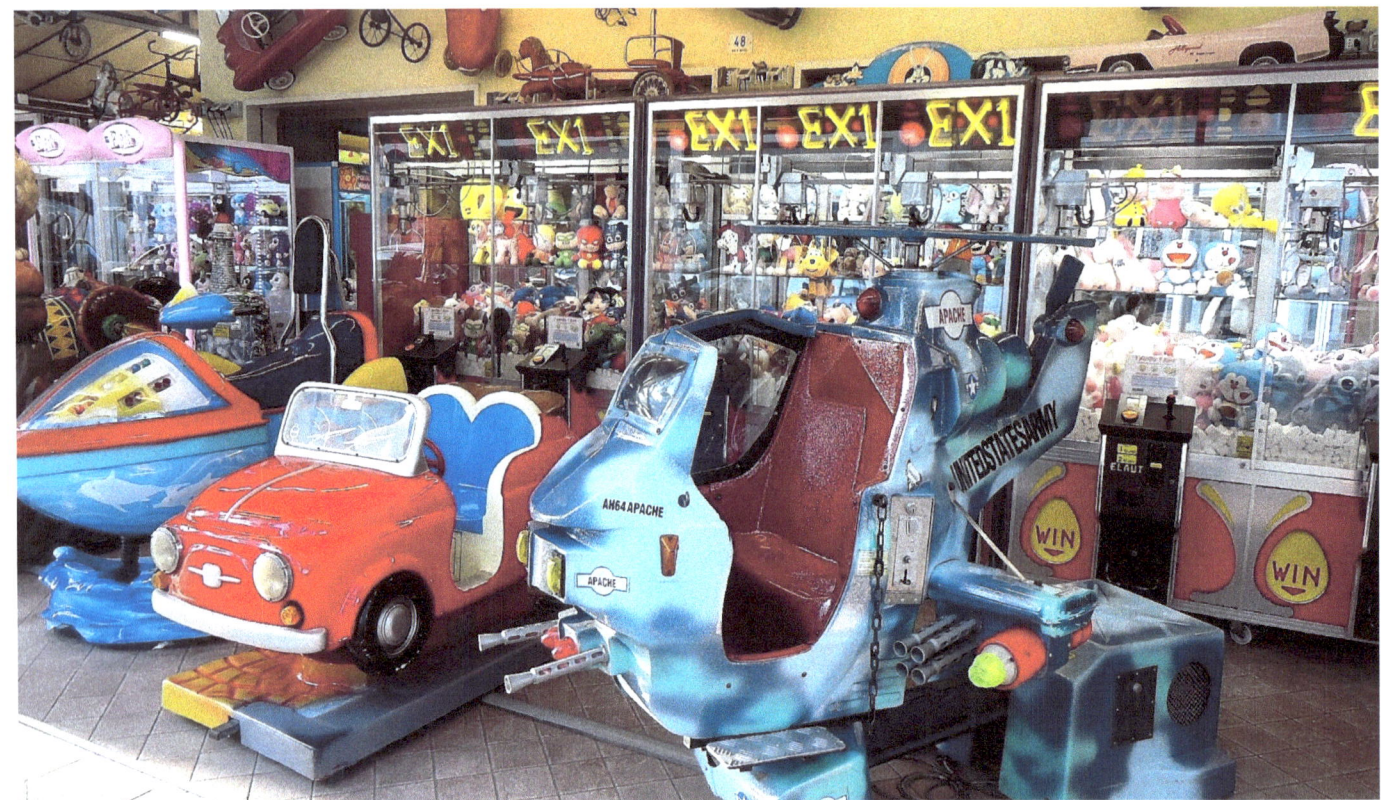

November

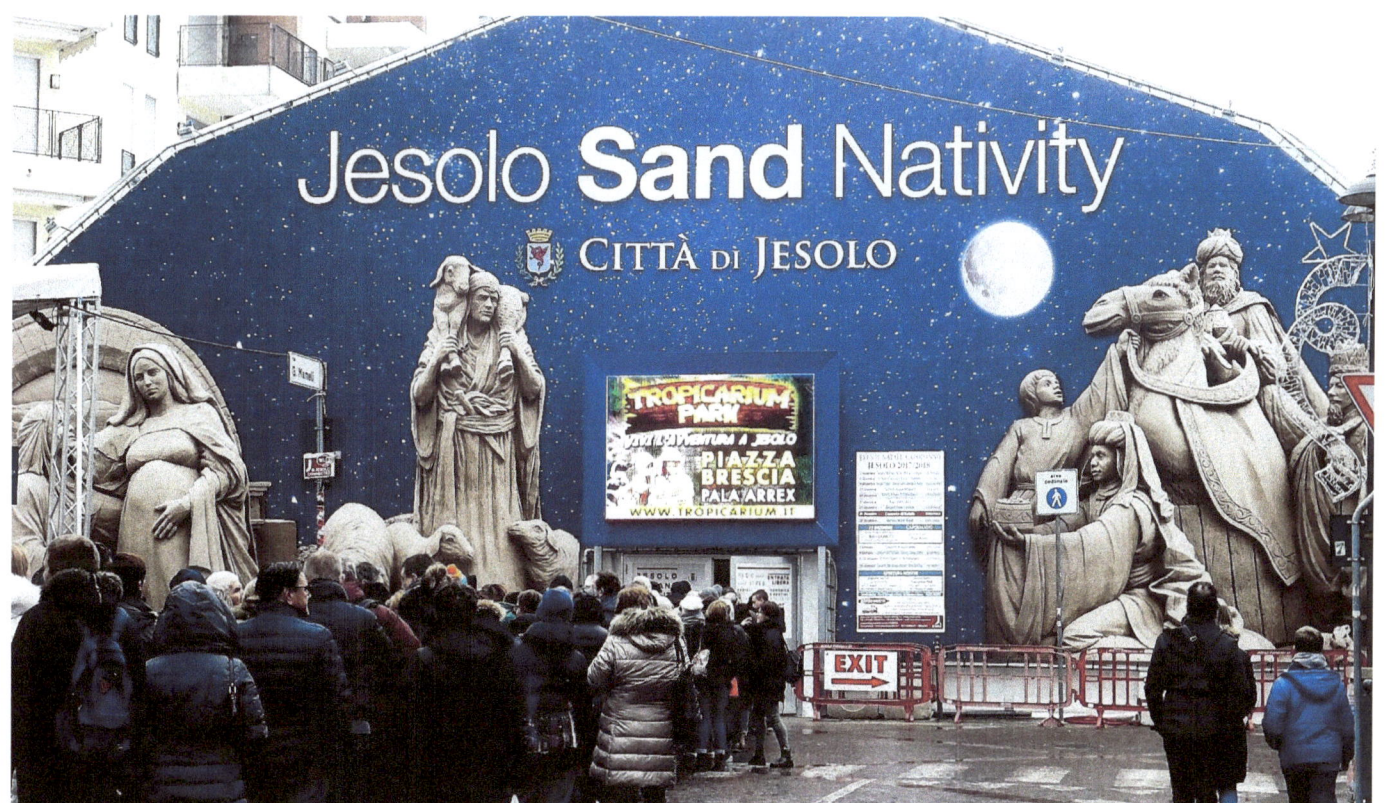

December

www.ingramcontent.com/pod-product-compliance
Lightning Source LLC
Chambersburg PA
CBHW051207220526
45473CB00003B/939